Pearson

Pearson Edexcel GCSE

German

Vocabulary, Grammar and Translation Workbook

Gabriela Hallas and Lisa Probert

Published by Pearson Education Limited, 80 Strand, London, WC2R ORL.

www.pearsonschoolsandfecolleges.co.uk

Copies of official specifications for all Pearson qualifications may be found on the website: qualifications.pearson.com

Edited and typeset by Newgen KnowledgeWorks

Original design by Kamae Design

Original illustrations © Pearson Education Limited 2025

Illustrated by Beehive Illustrations (Afua Bediako, Tamara Joubert, Andy Keylock, Daniel Limón, Mauro Marchesi, Andrew Pagram) and Newgen KnowledgeWorks

Cover design by Kamae Design

Cover photo and banner extract © FatCamera/Getty Images

Written by Gabriela Hallas and Lisa Probert

Select content created using AI based on Pearson learning materials. To maintain the integrity of content in this product, Pearson has a process to validate output prior to publication.

Printed in the UK by Bell & Bain Ltd, Glasgow

First published 2025

29 28 27 26 25

10 9 8 7 6 5 4 3 2 1

British Library Cataloguing in Publication Data

A catalogue record for this book is available from the British Library

ISBN 978 1 292 489568

Notes from the publisher
Pearson has robust editorial processes, including answer and fact checks, to ensure the accuracy of the content in this publication, and every effort is made to ensure this publication is free of errors. We are, however, only human, and occasionally errors do occur. Pearson is not liable for any misunderstandings that arise as a result of errors in this publication, but it is our priority to ensure that the content is accurate. If you spot an error, please do contact us at resourcescorrections@pearson.com so we can make sure it is corrected.

Inhalt

Basic language

1 Translate these everyday words and phrases into English.

1 ja ....

2 nein ....

3 nicht ....

4 okay ....

5 Hallo! ....

6 Guten Tag! ....

7 Auf Wiedersehen! ....

2 Fill in the missing subject pronouns.

German	*ich*	....	*er*	....	*es*	....	*wir*	....	....	*sie*
English	I	you (sg)	he	she	....	one/you/we	....	you (plural)	you (formal, sg and pl)	....

3 Write the German words for the days of the week in the correct order, starting with Monday.

Sonntag Mittwoch Freitag Montag Samstag Donnerstag Dienstag

....

....

4 Draw lines to match up the German seasons with the correct pictures.

1 der Frühling **2** der Sommer **3** der Herbst **4** der Winter

a

b

c

d

5 Fill in the missing letters in the German months of the year.

1 Jan_ar

2 Fe_ruar

3 M_rz

4 April

5 Ma_

6 Jun_

7 Jul_

8 August

9 September

10 O_tober

11 November

12 De_ember

6 Fill in the missing number words in German.

1 ...., eins, zwei, ..., vier, fünf, ..., sieben, acht, neun

2 ...., ..., dreizehn, vierzehn, fünfzehn, sechzehn, ..., achtzehn, neunzehn

3 ...., zwanzig, ..., vierzig, ..., sechzig, siebzig, achtzig, ...

4 hundert, ..., Million

G

To form **ordinal numbers** in German, add ***-te*** to numbers 1 to 19, and ***-ste*** to numbers 20 and higher.
*der/die/das zwei**te**/vier**te**/fünf**te***
the second/fourth/fifth
*der/die/das zwanzig**ste**/hundert**ste***
the twentieth/hundredth
Exceptions are *der/die/das* ***erste*** (the first), ***dritte*** (third), *sie**bte*** (seventh).

G

To say the date in German, use the preposition ***am*** followed by the ordinal number with ***-ten*** on the end for 1st to 19th, and ***-sten*** on the end for 21st to 31st.
am ersten*/zwei**ten**/**siebten** August*
on the first/second/seventh of August
***am** einundzwanzig**sten**/dreißig**sten** September*
on the twenty-first/thirtieth of September

These German words will be useful: *Silvester, Karneval.*

7 Translate these sentences into German.

1 Saturday is the ninth of October.

....

2 Friday is the twentieth of February.

....

3 Carnival is on the eleventh of March.

....

4 New Year's Eve is on the thirty-first of December.

....

8 Fill in the missing colour words in German.

1 Die Hose ist .... (*blue*) und das Hemd ist .... (*yellow*).
2 Der Rock ist .... (*brown*) und die Jacke ist .... (*green*).
3 Der Pullover ist .... (*grey*) und .... (*pink*).
4 Die Schuhe sind .... (*red*) und .... (*orange*).
5 Die Katze ist .... (*black*) und .... (*white*).

9 Match up the German words that relate to places and culture (1–9) with their English translations (a–i). Write the correct letter.

1 Afrika ....
2 Amerika ....
3 Asien ....
4 die Türkei ....
5 die Schweiz ....
6 die Donau ....
7 der Rhein ....
8 der Kanton ....
9 die Viennale ....

a Switzerland
b Africa
c canton
d Asia
e Turkey
f Vienna International Film Festival
g the Danube
h the Rhine
i America

10 Separate the words and write out the German sentences about places.

1 berlin,kölnundmünchensindindeutschland ....
2 wienistinösterreich ....
3 großbritannienistineuropa ....

Kulturzone Meine Schule, deine Schule

Using articles and plural nouns

1 Draw lines to match up the German words with their English translations.

1 die Jugendlichen	**a** classroom
2 das Kind	**b** homework
3 die Schülerin	**c** child
4 der Lehrer	**d** (female) pupil
5 das Klassenzimmer	**e** (male) teacher
6 die Hausaufgaben	**f** young people
7 der Trainer	**g** coach

2 Circle the noun in each sentence, then translate the nouns into English.

1 Wir haben viele Ferien. ....

2 Der typische Schultag beginnt früh. ....

3 Das ist eine Klasse. ....

4 Wir haben keine Uniform. ....

5 Das ist das britische Schulsystem. ....

H 6 Meine gesamte Schule ist gut. ....

Some **nouns** are made from two words. For example, ***Schulsystem*** is a compound of *Schule* + *System*.

3 Fill in the missing indefinite articles.

1 Er hat .... Buch (*nt*).

2 Sie kauft sowohl .... Heft (*nt*) als auch ein Buch.

3 Wir bekommen .... Computer (*m*).

4 Ihr kauft .... Wasserflasche (*f*).

5 Sie haben .... Kuli (*m*).

6 Bekommst du .... Schultasche (*f*)?

G The **indefinite article** is translated as 'a' or 'an'. It changes depending on whether the noun that follows is masculine, feminine or neuter.

Nominative

masculine	feminine	neuter
ein	eine	ein

Accusative

masculine	feminine	neuter
ein**en**	eine	ein

4 Circle the definite article in each sentence. Write if it is masculine (m), feminine (f), neuter (nt) or plural (pl).

1 Der Schultag dauert von 7:30 bis 13:00 Uhr. ....

2 Die Ferien dauern zehn Wochen. ....

3 Die Hausaufgaben dauern zwei bis drei Stunden. ....

4 Hier ist das deutsche Schulsystem. ....

H 5 Hier ist eigentlich der Direktor. ....

H 6 Zu Schulbeginn bekommt sie die große Schultüte. ....

G The **definite article** is translated as 'the'. It changes depending on whether the noun that follows is masculine, feminine, neuter or plural.

Nominative

masculine	feminine	neuter	plural
der	die	das	die

Accusative

masculine	feminine	neuter	plural
den	die	das	die

G

Nouns form their **plural** in different ways in German.
Here are some of the most common ways.

	what changes	singular	plural
masculine	adds -*s* stays the same	der Kuli der Computer	die Kulis die Computer
feminine	adds -*n*	die Schultasche	die Schultaschen
neuter	adds -*e* adds umlaut and -*er*	das Heft das Buch	die Hefte die Bücher

5 Write the plural forms of these words.

1 die Wasserflasche ....

2 das Angebot ....

3 die Liste ....

4 der Test ....

H 5 die Schultüte ....

H 6 die Note ....

F 6 Translate these sentences into English.

1 Alle Schüler tragen eine Schuluniform.

....

2 Sie hat ein altes Buch und ein neues Heft.

....

3 Ihr bekommt einen Computer.

....

4 Sie bleiben im Klassenzimmer.

....

5 Wo machst du die Hausaufgaben?

....

H 7 Translate this paragraph into German.

We are comparing school systems. In England everyone mostly wears school uniform but we have no uniforms. At the start of school, they receive a book list and exercise books. In Germany we have lots of tests. Here the teachers teach five lessons a day.

....

....

....

....

....

1 Wie ist dein Stundenplan dieses Jahr?

Using the present tense • Using *weil*

1 Circle the odd one out.

1 Mathe Englisch Stunde Deutsch

2 Geschichte Sport Mittagessen Religion

3 Musik Kunst Theater Wissenschaft

4 interessant wichtig schwierig nützlich

H 5 Mittwoch Stundenplan Samstag Montag

H 6 Buch Kuli Aufgabe Heft

	Montag	Dienstag	Mittwoch	Donnerstag	Freitag
1. Stunde	Mathe	Chemie	Englisch	Deutsch	Physik
2. Stunde	Biologie	Englisch	Mathe	Englisch	Chemie
			Pause		
3. Stunde	Deutsch	Französisch	Geschichte	Kunst	Theater
4. Stunde	Englisch	Kunst	Deutsch	Spanisch	Mathe
5. Stunde	Erdkunde	Informatik	Religion	Musik	Biologie
			Mittagspause		
6. Stunde	Musik	Sport	Physik	Sport	Französisch

2 Translate the underlined phrases into English.

1 Das Mittagessen ist um zwölf Uhr. ....

2 Am Nachmittag habe ich Sport. ....

3 In der ersten Stunde habe ich Mathe. ....

4 In der zweiten Stunde habe ich Kunst. ....

5 Dreimal pro Woche habe ich Deutsch. ....

H 6 Zu Beginn spreche ich mit meinen Freundinnen. ....

3 Write the correct present tense form of the verb in brackets.

1 Er .... die Hausaufgaben. (*machen*)

2 Sie (*They*) .... Hefte. (*bekommen*)

3 Es .... eine Stunde. (*dauern*)

4 Wir .... die Schulsysteme. (*vergleichen*)

5 Ihr .... Handball. (*spielen*)

6 Du .... um zwei Uhr. (*beginnen*)

G

The **present tense** of regular verbs is formed by adding endings to the stem. Start with the infinitive and take off *-en* to get the stem. Then add the endings below:

lernen (*to learn*)
ich lern**e**
du lern**st**
er/sie/es/man lern**t**
wir lern**en**
ihr lern**t**
Sie lern**en**
sie lern**en**

4 Write the correct form of *haben* or *sein* to complete each sentence.

1 Wir .... alle Schüler und Schülerinnen.

2 Sie (*They*) .... gut in Mathe.

3 Ihr .... ein Heft.

4 Du .... schwach in Kunst.

5 Ich .... ein Buch.

H 6 Die Aufgabe .... langweilig.

H 7 Gerade nach der Pause .... wir Wissenschaften.

G

Haben and ***sein*** are mostly irregular in the present tense.

	haben (*to have*)	**sein** (*to be*)
ich	habe	bin
du	hast	bist
er/sie/es/man	hat	ist
wir	haben	sind
ihr	habt	seid
Sie	haben	sind
sie	haben	sind

5 Rearrange the words to create correct sentences.

1 habe ich Deutsch In der dritten Stunde

....

2 Zweimal ich lerne pro Woche Englisch

....

3 Ich Mathe, weil leicht mag ist das

....

4 nicht, Kunst weil das ist schwierig mag Ich

....

H 5 mag meinen Stundenplan nicht, Ich weil er ist schwer

....

H 6 Ich gern Geschichte, weil nützlich ist lerne das

....

A **time phrase** comes first in a sentence, and then the **verb** comes second. For examples, look at exercise 2. What comes after each underlined time phrase?

G

Some **conjunctions** send the verb to the end of the clause. ***Weil* (because)** is an example of one of these conjunctions. There is always a comma before *weil*:

*Ich mag Deutsch, **weil** ich es interessant **finde**.*

I like German **because** I **find** it interesting.

F 6 Translate these sentences into German.

1 My favourite subject is German.

....

2 We begin at 8 a.m.

....

3 I like art because it's practical.

....

4 Once a week we have sport.

....

5 In the break I eat with friends.

....

H 7 Translate this paragraph into English.

Das ist mein Stundenplan. Viermal pro Woche habe ich Mathe. Wann hast du Englisch? Ich mag Geschichte lernen, aber Theater lerne ich überhaupt nicht gern. Kunst ist mein Lieblingsfach und ich mache Musik zu Hause. Sport ist schwer und ermüdend. Ich finde Wissenschaften wichtig, weil sie nützlich sind.

....

....

....

....

....

....

2 Was trägst du in der Schule?

Using adjectives with nouns • Using some irregular verbs

1 Match the words to the pictures. Write the correct letter.

1 die Schuhe .... 3 der Rock .... 5 die Jacke ....

2 das Kleid .... 4 die Hose .... 6 das Hemd ....

a
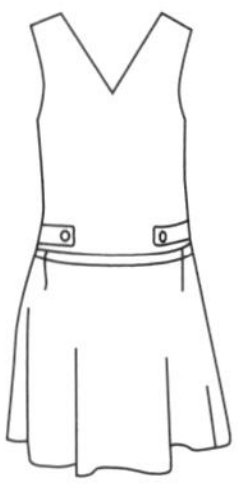
b

c
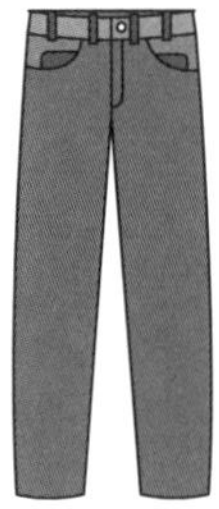
d
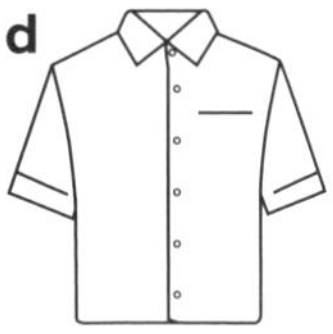
e

f

2 Choose the correct colour(s) from the box to complete each sentence.

rot	gelb
rosarot	grün
orange	blau
schwarz	weiß
grau	braun

1 Das T-Shirt ist .... (*yellow*)

2 Die Schuhe sind .... und .... (*green / white*)

3 Die Hose ist .... (*blue*)

4 Das Hemd ist .... und .... (*red / orange*)

5 Der Rock ist .... und .... (*black / grey*)

6 Die Jacke ist .... (*pink*)

3 Fill in the gaps with the correct form of the adjective in brackets.

1 Ich trage eine .... Krawatte. (*gelb*)

2 Ich habe einen .... Rock an. (*blau*)

3 Wir tragen .... Schuhe. (*schwarz*)

4 Die Jungen im Hintergrund tragen eine .... Hose, aber keine Jacke. (*hellgrau*)

5 Die Mädchen vorne tragen ein .... Hemd oder einen .... Pullover. (*weiß*)

6 Sie hat eine .... Jacke an. (*dunkelbraun*)

G

We use **adjectives** to describe things. When we put the adjective before the noun, it has to agree with the gender of the noun by taking the following endings.

Ich trage	ein**en**/kein**en**	blau**en**	Pullover.
	eine/keine	blau**e**	Krawatte.
	ein/kein	blau**es**	Hemd.
	–	blau**e**	Schuhe.
	keine	blau**en**	

ein(e)(n) means 'a'/'an'.
kein(e)(n) means 'not a' / 'not any' / 'no' (e.g. I am **not** wearing a blue jumper).

anhaben *to have on*

4 Complete the translations into German.

1 Ich trage .... (*brown shoes*).

2 Ich habe .... (*a blue dress*) an.

3 Er hat .... (*red trousers*) an.

4 Sie trägt .... (*a black hat*).

5 Wir tragen .... (*a dark green T-shirt*).

6 Sie tragen .... (*a light yellow tie*).

5 Fill in the gaps with the correct present tense form of the verb in brackets.

1 Wir .... mit dem Bus. (*fahren*)

2 Er .... sechzehn Stunden pro Tag. (*schlafen*)

3 Die Jungen .... sowohl ein graues Hemd als auch einen schwarzen Pullover. (*tragen*)

4 .... du gut? (*schlafen*)

5 Der Lehrer .... mit dem Rad. (*fahren*)

6 .... ihr Kleidung in Mode? (*tragen*)

G

Some verbs, such as ***tragen* (to wear)**, add an umlaut in the *du* and *er/sie/es/man* forms of the present tense.

tragen (*to wear*)	
ich	trage
du	tr**ä**gst
er/sie/es/man	tr**ä**gt
wir	tragen
ihr	tragt
Sie	tragen
sie	tragen

Some other verbs that follow the same pattern are:
fahren (to drive, go):
ich fahre → *du fährst*
schlafen (to sleep):
ich schlafe → *er schläft*

F 6 Translate these sentences into English.

You may know that *im Hintergrund* means 'in the background'. So what do you think *im Vordergrund* means?

1 Was gibt es auf dem Foto?

....

2 Auf dem Foto sieht man eine Lehrerin.

....

3 Im Vordergrund gibt es einen Jungen.

....

4 Das Mädchen vorne trägt eine schwarze Hose.

....

5 Welche Farbe magst du?

....

H 7 Translate this paragraph into German.

In the background there is a girl. She is wearing a light green and white dress. She is eating chips. In the foreground you see a second girl. She has a dark grey jumper and a black skirt on. They are wearing brown shoes but the fashion is white shoes.

....

....

....

....

....

....

3 Sind Schulregeln wirklich nötig?

Using modal verbs: *müssen, dürfen, sollen* • Using opinion phrases with *dass*

1 Find the places in the school on the plan. Write the correct letter.

1 der Musikraum ....
2 das Klassenzimmer ....
3 der Gang ....
4 die Bibliothek ....
5 der Computerraum ....

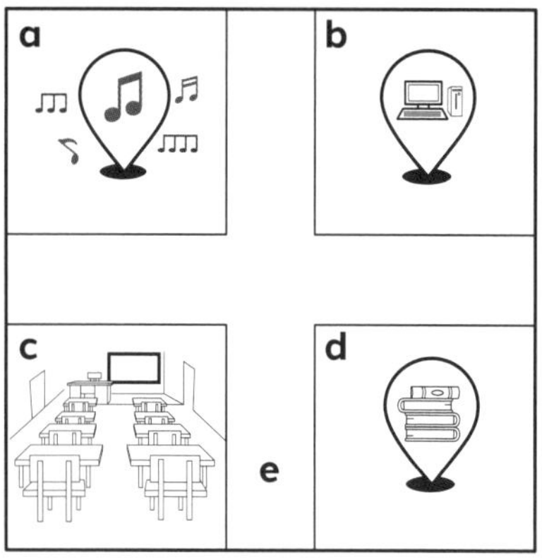

2 Translate these English infinitives into German.

1 to show ....
2 to do, make ....
3 to eat ....
4 to drink ....
5 to talk ....
H 6 to chat ....

3 Complete these sentences with the correct form of the verb in brackets.

1 Du wirfst ein Heft, aber man .... nicht gefährliche Sachen machen. (*sollen*)
2 Du benutzt dein Handy, aber man .... den Text lesen. (*sollen*)
3 Du sprichst, aber man .... im Unterricht nicht reden. (*dürfen*)
4 Man .... im Computerraum nicht trinken, weil das nicht erlaubt ist. (*dürfen*)
5 Man .... in der Bibliothek leise sein. (*müssen*)
6 Man .... draußen Fußball spielen und im Gang nicht laufen. (*sollen*)

G

We use **modal verbs** to talk about what we are allowed to do, what we must do and what we should do.

	dürfen (*to be allowed to, may*)	**müssen** (*to have to, must*)	**sollen** (*to be supposed to, should*)
ich	darf	muss	soll
du	darfst	musst	sollst
er/sie/es/man	darf	muss	soll
wir	dürfen	müssen	sollen

4 Complete the sentences using a verb from the box.

1 Man soll in der Bibliothek leise ....
2 Man muss das Handy zu Hause ....
3 Man darf seine Hausaufgaben nicht ....
H 4 Wir müssen die Hausaufgaben ....
H 5 Wir dürfen für den Mathetest ....
H 6 Wir sollen im Unterricht nicht ....

sein	sprechen	lassen
lernen	machen	vergessen

G

When we use modal verbs, the second verb of the sentence is always in the **infinitive form** and goes to the end of the clause or sentence.

5 Write full sentences by linking the two parts with *dass*.

> **G** The **conjunction *dass* (that)** sends the verb to the end of the clause, like *weil* does. There is always a comma before *dass*.

1 Ich glaube / Diese Regel ist sehr schlecht.

....

....

2 Ich denke / Diese Regel ist ziemlich gut.

....

3 Ich finde / Diese Regel ist nicht wichtig.

....

4 Ich glaube / Es ist richtig. ....

5 Ich finde / Es ist falsch. ....

6 Ich denke / Es ist nicht notwendig.

....

F 6 Translate these sentences into German.

1 He has to be quiet in class.

....

2 You aren't allowed to eat in the computer room.

....

3 Why do you find it so wrong?

....

4 It's very uncomfortable in the library.

....

5 I find this rule very practical and important.

....

H 7 Translate this paragraph into English.

Ich bin der Meinung, dass ich nicht genug Freizeit habe. Man muss jeden Abend mindestens drei Stunden Hausaufgaben machen und das ist zu viel. Man darf sein Handy im Klassenzimmer nicht benutzen. Ich denke, dass diese Regel total falsch und wirklich nicht notwendig ist. Wir müssen eine Schuluniform tragen – ich kann meinen Charakter nicht zeigen.

....

....

....

....

....

....

4 Schultage: die beste Zeit deines Lebens?

Using the perfect and imperfect tenses

1 Translate these compound nouns into English.

1 Sporttag ....

2 Modewoche ....

3 Theaterstück ....

4 Klassenfahrt ....

5 Freizeitpark ....

H 6 Schulausflug ....

Remember to separate compound nouns into their component parts to help work out the meaning.

2 Write the English translation of the German infinitives. Then draw lines to match each German infinitive with its past participle.

	Infinitive	Past participle
1	schwimmen	gegangen
2	fahren	gegessen
3	essen	gekauft
4	kaufen	geschwommen
5	fliegen	gefahren
6	gehen	geflogen

3 Circle the correct form of the auxiliary verb to complete each sentence.

1 Ich **bin** / **habe** / **bist** zehn Kilometer zu Fuß gegangen.

2 Er **hat** / **haben** / **ist** im Schwimmbad geschwommen.

3 Ich **habe** / **bin** / **habt** meine Kunsthausaufgabe gezeigt.

4 Sie **sind** / **haben** / **seid** etwas zum Essen gekauft.

5 Ich **habe** / **ist** / **bin** mit dem Bus gefahren.

6 Du **sind** / **seid** / **bist** zu Hause geblieben.

G To form the **perfect tense** you need an **auxiliary verb**. This can be the present tense of *haben* or *sein*. We always use *sein* for verbs of movement like *gehen* (to go) and *schwimmen* (to swim).

4 Fill in the gaps with the past participle of the verb in brackets. Some are irregular.

1 Ich habe ein Musical .... (*machen*)

2 Er hat die Hauptrolle .... (*spielen*)

3 Du bist einkaufen .... (*gehen*)

4 Er ist mit uns in den Freizeitpark .... (*kommen*)

5 Ihr habt Pommes .... (*essen*)

6 Wir haben in einem Musical .... (*singen*)

G To form the **past participle** of regular verbs, take off *-en* from the infinitive, and add *ge-* to the front of the stem and *-t* to the end of the stem. For example:
hören ⟶ *gehört*
Some verbs have irregular past participles and you will need to learn these.

Haupt-	*main*
Hauptrolle (*f*)	*main role*

G

We use the **imperfect tense** to say what something **was/ used to be** like or what someone **had/ used to have**.

	sein (*to be*)	**haben** (*to have*)
ich	war	hatte
du	warst	hattest
er/sie/es/man	war	hatte
wir	waren	hatten
ihr	wart	hattet
Sie	waren	hatten
sie	waren	hatten

5 Fill in the gaps with the correct imperfect tense form of *haben* or *sein*.

1 Die Busfahrt .... 16 Kilometer lang.

2 Ich .... so viele Fragen.

3 Wie .... der Freizeitpark?

4 Ich .... glücklich, weil der Tag fantastisch war.

H 5 Sie *(They)* .... froh, weil sie *(they)* in der Schule ein Konzert ....

H 6 Der Schulausflug ist jetzt vorbei, aber wir .... viel Spaß.

F **6 Translate these sentences into English.**

1 Letzte Woche bin ich einkaufen gegangen.

....

2 Ich habe Musikinstrumente im Konzert gespielt.

....

3 Letztes Jahr bin ich zwanzig Kilometer zu Fuß gegangen.

....

4 Gestern hat sie interessante Sachen gemacht.

....

5 Wir waren glücklich, weil das Wetter gut war.

....

H **7 Translate this paragraph into German.**

Last week there was a fashion week and I showed great clothes. My friend did a musical and played the main role. We all did very interesting things and we learned a lot. The teacher swam twenty kilometres. It was a very practical week and we had lots of fun.

....

....

....

....

....

5 Austausch geht auch online!

- Using the present tense with a future time phrase
- Speaking and writing in the past and present

1 Fill in the missing English or German translations.

	a minute		a week	a year
eine Sekunde	*eine Minute*	*eine Stunde*		

2 Draw lines to match up the questions and answers.

1 Kannst du deine Schule beschreiben?
2 Was machst du in der Pause?
3 Was hast du gestern nach der Schule gemacht?
4 Was machst du heute nach der Schule?
5 Wie viele Stunden habt ihr pro Tag?

a Ich bin nach Hause gegangen.
b Sie ist ziemlich groß.
c Heute gehe ich in die Stadt.
d Wir haben fünf Stunden.
e Ich verbringe oft Zeit mit Freunden.

3 Rewrite the English translations, correcting the error(s).

1 Heute Abend gehe ich in einen Klub. *This evening I'm meeting in a club.*

....

....

2 Morgen trifft er einen Freund. *Tomorrow he's eating with a friend.*

....

3 Heute in der Pause esse ich Pommes. *Today at breaktime I want to eat chips.*

....

4 Morgen stehe ich um sieben Uhr auf. *Tomorrow I got up at seven o'clock.*

....

5 Heute nach der Schule spiele ich entweder Tennis oder Fußball. *Today after school I played either tennis or football.*

....

G You can use the **present tense** to talk about the future, by using future time phrases:
Heute nach der Schule rede ich *mit meinen Eltern.*
Today after school I'm talking to my parents.

4 Use these phrases to write sentences starting with a time phrase.

1 ich / lerne / Tennis / normalerweise

....

....

2 ich / mache / meine Hausaufgaben / jeden Tag

....

3 ich / mit Freunden / esse / morgen in der Pause

....

G The **verb** is usually the **second idea** in a German sentence. If you start with a time phrase, the **verb** and the subject change places.
Ich ***treibe*** *Sport.* → *Heute* ***treibe*** *ich Sport.*
Ich ***habe*** *Pommes gegessen.* → *In der Pause* ***habe*** *ich Pommes gegessen.*

H **4** ich / kein Mittagessen essen / gestern in der Pause

....

H **5** er / zu viel Zeit verbringen / im Klassenzimmer / letztes Jahr

....

H **6** ich / mit Freunden / reden / jede Woche

....

H **5 Fill in the missing verbs to complete the German sentences so that they make sense.**

Think about which tense is indicated by the time expression. You may need a present, a perfect or an imperfect tense verb.

1 Wir .... oft Fußball.

2 Gestern .... ich Sport ....

Es .... spannend.

3 Letzte Woche .... ich viel ...., weil ich so müde ....

4 Jede Woche .... ich in einen Klub. Letzte Woche aber .... ich keine Zeit.

F **6 Translate these sentences into German.**

1 I am describing my school.

....

2 The maths lesson lasts fifty minutes.

....

3 Are you meeting your exchange partner?

....

4 I spend time with friends.

....

5 It's good that school finishes early.

....

H **7 Translate this paragraph into English.**

Der Titel von dieser Aufgabe ist ‚Wie ist deine Schule?' Es gibt ungefähr sechshundert Schüler und Schülerinnen in meinem Gymnasium. Letztes Jahr gab es zu viele Hausaufgaben, aber dieses Jahr ist es besser, weil sie nicht so schwer oder langweilig sind. Ich finde, dass die Schuluniform sowohl ein Vorteil als auch ein Nachteil ist.

....

....

....

....

....

Glossary

bold = this word will appear in Higher exams only

aber	*but, however*
alle	*everyone, everybody (pl)*
alt	*old*
Angebot (nt)	*offer*
anhaben	*(to) wear, have on | wearing, having on*
Aufgabe (f)	*task, assignment, exercise*
aufstehen	*(to) get up, stand up | getting up, standing up*
Austausch (m)	*exchange*
Beginn (m); zu Beginn	*beginning; in the beginning*
beginnen	*(to) begin, start | beginning, starting*
bekommen	*(to) receive, get | receiving, getting*
beschreiben	*(to) describe | describing*
Bibliothek (f)	*library*
bin	*(I) am | am being*
bleiben	*(to) stay, remain | staying, remaining*
britisch	*British*
Buch (nt)	*book*
Club/Klub (m)	*club*
Computer (m)	*computer*
darf	*(I) am allowed to, may | (she, he, it, one) is allowed to, may*
darfst	*(you (sing informal)) are allowed to, may*
das	*the (nt)*
dass	*that*
dauern	*(to) last | lasting*
denken	*(to) think | thinking*
der	*the (m)*
deutsch	*German*
die	*the (f), the (pl)*
diese	*these, those (pl)*
Direktor (m)	*headteacher, director*
dritt	*third*
dunkel	*dark*
dürfen	*(to) be allowed to, may*
eigentlich	*actual, actually, in fact*
ein	*a/an (m, nt)*
eine	*a/an (f)*
einem	*(to/for) one (indirect obj)*
einen	*one (obj)*
einkaufen	*(to) shop | shopping*
einmal	*once, one time*
englisch	*English*
entweder	*either*
erlauben	*(to) allow | allowing*
erst	*first*
es (...) gab	*there was | there were | there used to be*
es (...) gibt	*there is | there are*
essen	*(to) eat | eating*
etwas	*something, some, a little*
Fach (nt)	*subject*
fahren	*(to) go (by transport), drive, travel | going, driving, travelling*
fantastisch	*fantastic, fantastically*
Farbe (f)	*colour, paint*
finden	*(to) find | finding*
Flasche (f)	*bottle*

Foto (nt)	*photograph*
Frage (f)	*question*
froh	*happy, glad*
Fußball (m)/ Fussball	*football*
Gang (m)	*corridor, course*
gerade	*straight, just*
gesamt	*whole, entire, comprehensive*
Geschichte (f)	*history, story*
gestern	*yesterday*
glauben	*(to) think, believe | thinking, believing*
gut	*good*
haben	*(to) have | having*
hat	*(she, he, it, one) has | is having*
hatten	*(we/they/you (formal)) had | used to have | were having*
hattest	*(you (sing informal)) had | used to have | were having*
hattet	*(you (pl informal)) had | used to have | were having*
Haupt-	*main*
Hausaufgabe (f)	*homework*
Heft (nt)	*workbook, exercise book*
hell	*light*
Hemd (nt)	*shirt*
Hintergrund (m)	*background*
Hose (f)	*trousers*
Hut (m)	*hat*
Instrument (nt)	*instrument*
isst	*(you (sing informal)) eat | are eating | (she, he, it, one) eats | is eating*
Jacke (f)	*jacket*
Jahr (nt)	*year*
(die) Jugendliche(n) (pl)	*(the) young people*
(der/die) Jugendliche	*(the) young person, teenager*
(ein(e)) Jugendliche(r) (m/f)	*(a) young person, teenager*
Junge (m)	*boy*
kannst	*(you (sing informal)) are able to, can*
kaufen	*(to) buy | buying*
kein	*not a, no (m, nt)*
keine	*not a (f), not any, no (f, pl)*
Kilometer (m)	*kilometre*
Kind (nt)	*child*
Klasse (f)	*class, year (in school)*
Kleid (nt)	*dress*
Krawatte (f)	*tie*
Kuli (m)	*pen*
Kunst (f)	*art*
langweilig	*boring*
lassen	*(to) let, allow, leave | letting, allowing, leaving*
laufen	*(to) run | running*
leicht	*easy, light*
leise	*quiet, quietly, soft, softly*
lernen	*(to) learn | learning*
letzt-(er, e, es), letzte	*last (m, f, nt), (pl)*
Lieblings-	*favourite*
Liste (f)	*list*
machen	*(to) do, make | doing, making*
Mädchen (nt)	*girl*
Mathe(matik) (f)	*maths*
mein	*my (m, nt)*

meine	*my (f, pl)*
meistens	*mostly*
Minute (f)	*minute*
Mittagessen (nt)	*lunch*
Mode (f)	*fashion*
Musical (nt)	*musical*
Musik (f)	*music*
muss	*(I) have to, must | am having to | (she, he, it, one) has to, must | is having to*
müssen	*(to) have to, must | having to*
musst	*(you (sing informal)) have to, must | are having to*
nach Hause	*home; to (your) home*
Nachmittag (m)	*afternoon*
Nachteil (m)	*disadvantage, con*
normalerweise	*normally*
nötig	*necessary*
notwendig	*necessary, essential*
nützlich	*useful*
oder	*or*
oft	*often*
Park (m)	*park*
Pause (f)	*break*
plaudern	*(to) chat | chatting*
Pommes (frites) (pl)	*chips*
Pullover/Pulli (m)	*pullover, jumper*
Regel (f)	*rule*
Religion (f)	*religion*
richtig	*right, correct*
schlafen	*(to) sleep | sleeping*
schläfst	*(you (sing informal)) sleep | are sleeping*
schläft	*(she, he, it, one) sleeps | is sleeping*
Schuh (m)	*shoe*
Schule (f)	*school*
Schüler (m)	*pupil, student (school)*
schwer	*heavy, difficult*
schwierig	*hard, difficult*
sehr	*very*
sein; **sich (dat) ... sein**	*(to) be | being;* ***(to) feel | feeling***
Sekunde (f)	*second*
siehst	*(you (sing informal)) see, watch, look | are seeing, watching, looking*
sieht	*(she, he, it, one) sees, watches, looks | is seeing, watching, looking*
sind	*(we/they/you (formal)) are | are being*
so	*so, thus, in this way, such*
soll	*(I) ought to, am supposed to, should | (she, he, it, one) ought to, is supposed to, should*
sollst	*(you (sing informal)) ought to, are supposed to, should*
sowohl ... als auch ...	*both ... and ...*
Spaß (m)	*fun*
spielen	*(to) play | playing*
Sport (m)	*sport*

sprechen	*(to) speak | speaking*
sprichst	*(you (sing informal)) speak | are speaking*
spricht	*(she, he, it, one) speaks | is speaking*
Stundenplan (m)	*timetable*
System (nt)	*system*
Tag (m)	*day*
Test (m)	*test*
Text (m)	*text*
Theater (nt)	*theatre, drama*
Titel (m)	*title*
total	*total, totally*
trägst	*(you (sing informal)) wear, carry | are wearing, carrying*
trägt	*(she, he, it, one) wears, carries | is wearing, carrying*
Trainer (m)	*coach*
triffst	*(you (sing informal)) meet | are meeting*
trifft	*(she, he, it, one) meets | is meeting*
trinken	*(to) drink | drinking*
T-Shirt (nt)	*t-shirt*
Tüte (f)	*bag*
typisch	*typical, typically*
überhaupt	*at all, generally*
und	*and*
ungefähr	*about, approximately*
Uniform (f)	*uniform*
Unterricht (m)	*lesson, teaching, instruction, classes*
unterrichten	*(to) teach | teaching*
verbringen	*(to) spend (time) | spending (time)*
vergleichen	*(to) compare | comparing*
viel	*a lot, much*
viele	*a lot, many*
vorbei	*past, over*
Vordergrund (m)	*foreground*
vorne	*at/to the front*
Vorteil (m)	*advantage, pro*
wann	*when(?)*
war	*(I, she, he, it, one) was | used to be*
waren	*(we/they/you (formal)) were | used to be*
warst	*(you (sing informal)) were | used to be*
wart	*(you (pl informal)) were | used to be*
warum	*why?*
was	*what(?), that*
weil	*because*
welch-(er, e, es), welche	*which (m, f, nt), (pl)*
wichtig	*important, importantly*
wie	*how(?)*
wirfst	*(you (sing informal)) throw | are throwing*
Wissenschaft (f)	*science*
wo	*where(?)*
Woche (f)	*week*
zeigen	*(to) show | showing*
Zeit (f)	*time*
ziemlich	*quite, fairly, pretty*
zweimal	*twice*
zweit	*second*

Kulturzone Kennst du diese Musiker?

Giving opinions • Using intensifiers and qualifiers

1 Unjumble the letters to rewrite the German intensifiers correctly. Then translate them into English.

1 uz ....

2 rhes ....

3 ebosnreds ....

4 zgna ....

5 lchikriwh ....

6 tihcn ....

7 chzimeil ....

2 Translate each word (a–e). Then complete each sentence (1–5) using one of the words (a–e).

a Sänger ....

b Fan ....

c Gruppe ....

d Lied ....

e Programm ....

> **G** You can use **intensifiers** and **qualifiers** to strengthen or weaken your adjectives. They usually go before the adjective.

1 Ich bin ein großer .... von Namika.

2 Herbert Grönemeyer ist der beste ....

3 Die Ärzte sind eine ....

4 Das .... ist sehr traurig.

H 5 Es gibt viele Sendungen auf diesem ....

3 Underline the intensifier and circle the adjective in each sentence. Then translate these words into English.

1 Das beliebte Lied ist sehr berühmt. ....

2 Seine Stimme ist besonders wunderbar. ....

3 Tanzmusik ist wirklich spannend. ....

4 Ich finde Popmusik zu langweilig. ....

5 Er ist ein ganz interessanter Star. ....

> **G** You can give your opinion by:
>
> - using an **opinion verb** such as *mögen*, *lieben* and *hassen*:
>   *Ich **mag** Popmusik.*
>   *Ich **liebe** Musikvideos.*
>   *Ich **hasse** Rockmusik.*
> - using an **adjective**:
>   *Das ist **ruhig**.*
>   *Dieses Lied ist **laut**.*
>   *Ich finde seine Lieder **traurig**.*

4 Rewrite each English translation, putting the words into the correct order.

1 Dieser Musiker ist wirklich bekannt.

well-known / this / is / musician / really ....

2 Klassische Musik kann ziemlich laut sein.

can / classical / loud / be / fairly / music ....

3 Ich mag Rockmusik, denn sie ist besonders modern.

rock music / I like / modern / particularly / because it is ....

4 Ich liebe diese Musik, denn sie ist sehr modisch.

because / I / fashionable / this music / it is / love / very ....

H 5 Sein Stil ist ganz schnell.

quick / his / quite / is / style ....

H 6 Das Publikum produziert eine sehr tolle Stimmung im Theater.

great / theatre / the / in the / atmosphere / produces / audience / a really

....

H 5 Correct the mistake in each English translation.

1 Diese Band singt sehr verrückte Lieder. *This band sings quite loud songs.*

....

2 Sein Lieblingslied ist ein Liebeslied. *His favourite song is a slow song.*

....

3 Ihr Ton ist auch wirklich ruhig. *Her tone is also really boring.*

....

4 Dieser Schauspieler singt sehr langsam. *This actor sings very badly.*

....

5 Sie ist eine völlig berühmte Sängerin. *She is not a completely famous singer.*

....

6 Letztes Jahr war er weltweit wirklich unbekannt. *Last year he was really happy worldwide.*

....

F 6 Translate these sentences into German.

1 I like classical music. ....
2 Pop music is particularly loud. ....
3 I love his voice because it's quite soft. ....
4 Yesterday we listened to rock music. ....
5 I hate this dance because it's too fast. ....

You can use ***denn*** or ***weil*** to translate 'because'.
Weil sends the <u>verb</u> to the end of the clause, but *denn* doesn't:
*Ich mag Popmusik, **denn** sie <u>ist</u> toll.*
*Ich mag Popmusik, **weil** sie toll <u>ist</u>.*

H 7 Translate this paragraph into English on a separate sheet.

Meine Lieblingssängerin ist toll, weil sie modern und modisch ist. Sie stammt aus Deutschland. Letzten Monat bin ich auf ein Konzert gegangen und sie hat auf Deutsch und auf Türkisch gesungen. Sie ist auch eine wirklich erfolgreiche Sängerin und ist in Deutschland überall bekannt. Ihre Musik klingt weder laut noch langweilig.

1 Was machst du gern in deiner Freizeit?

Using frequency phrases with correct word order

1 Translate the German infinitives into English.

1 lieben ....
5 wandern ....
9 tanzen ....
2 malen ....
6 sich interessieren ....
H 10 sich treffen ....
3 mögen ....
7 schwimmen ....
H 11 zeichnen ....
4 Radfahren ....
8 kochen ....

2 Underline the frequency expressions, then translate them into English.

1 Jedes Wochenende übe ich mein Gaming. ....
2 Ich tanze täglich. ....
3 Ab und zu gehe ich Radfahren. ....
4 Ich schwimme manchmal. ....
5 Ich male sehr oft. ....
H 6 Wöchentlich gehe ich wandern. ....

G

We can talk about how often we do things using **frequency expressions**. Here are some other examples:

am Wochenende at the weekend
jeden Tag every day
jede Woche every week
(fast) nie (almost) never
H *häufig* often
H *selten* seldom

Remember that when you use a frequency expression at the start of the sentence, the verb must stay in second position.

3 Rewrite each sentence using the frequency word or phrase in brackets.

1 Ich gehe ins Restaurant. (*manchmal*) ....
2 Ich treffe mich mit Freunden. (*oft*) ....
3 Ich lese die Zeitung. (*fast nie*) ....
4 Ich singe zu Hause. (*am Wochenende*) ....
5 Ich mache Sport in einem Schulklub. (*immer*) ....
H 6 Ich tanze in einem Verein. (*jede Woche*) ....

G

You can express preferences by:

- using the adverbs ***gern*** or ***lieber*** to qualify verbs:

Ich sehe sehr gern fern.
I like watching TV a lot.
Ich höre gar nicht gern Musik.
I really don't like listening to music.
Ich lese nicht gern. I don't like reading.
Ich tanze lieber. I prefer dancing.

- using the verb ***sich interessieren für*** **+ noun** to say what you are interested in:

Ich interessiere mich für Tanz.
I am interested in dance.
Ich interessiere mich nicht für Bücher.
I am not interested in books.

G

We use the **present tense** to talk about what we do regularly, or what we are doing.

regular verbs: malen (*to paint*)	**verbs with change to their vowel sounds in the *du* and *er/sie/es/man* forms: sehen** (*to see, watch, look*)
ich male	ich sehe
du malst	du s**ie**hst
er/sie/es/man malt	er/sie/es/man s**ie**ht
wir malen	wir sehen
ihr malt	ihr seht
Sie malen	Sie sehen
sie malen	sie sehen

4 Draw lines to match up the questions with the answers. Add an emoticon (✗, ♥ or ♥♥) next to each answer to show how much they like it.

1 Fährst du gern Rad?
2 Malst du gern?
3 Was machst du lieber, Schwimmen oder Wandern?
4 Wofür interessierst du dich?
5 Was machst du nicht gern?
6 Was liest du gern?

a Ich mache diese Übung nicht gern. ....
b Ich male gar nicht gern. ....
c Ich interessiere mich für Filme. ....
d Ich fahre nicht gern Rad. ....
e Ich lese sehr gern Romane. ....
f Ich gehe lieber wandern. ....

H 5 Rewrite each sentence, conjugating the verb in brackets and putting the words into the correct order.

1 ich / einkaufen / jedes Wochenende / (gehen) ....
2 (malen) / er / schöne / Bilder / liebsten / am ....
3 oft / (machen) / gern / wir / Fotos ....
4 Computer / (spielen) / gar nicht / am / ihr / gern ....
5 (besuchen) / deine Freunde / gern / du ....
6 sie (she) / Filme / gern / im Kino / (sehen) ....

F 6 Translate these sentences into English.

1 Ich treffe mich oft mit Freunden. ....
2 Er interessiert sich für Romane. ....
3 Ab und zu gehen wir wandern. ....
4 Sie fährt täglich Rad. ....
5 Ich lese nicht gern die Zeitung. ....

H 7 Translate this paragraph into German.

I like painting best of all. I paint and I draw every day. I dance in a club from time to time. I like dancing but I prefer doing sport. I seldom go hiking because I find it boring. I love reading but I almost never read the newspaper or novels.

....

....

....

....

....

....

2 Was machst du online?

Using separable verbs in the present tense

1 Write the words from the cloud in the correct column. Then write the English translations next to them.

benutzen, chatten, Handy, **H** Daten
Foto, Ding, schicken, **H** digital
sozial, rufen, Spieler, **H** elektronisch

Nouns	Adjectives	Verbs

2 Complete each sentence using a word from the box.

Passwort
Streaming
Nachrichten
Virus
Smartphone
Spielkonsole

1 Ich spiele oft auf der ....

2 Man muss ein starkes .... haben.

3 Ich schreibe nie ....

4 Man kann viele Probleme mit einem .... haben.

5 Ich finde .... toll, weil ich oft Musik höre.

6 Mit einem .... kann man alles machen.

3 Underline the two parts of the separable verb in each sentence.

1 Ich lade oft Videos hoch.

2 Rufst du deine Familie an?

3 Sie bringt immer ihr Laptop mit.

4 Seht ihr gern fern?

5 Wir laden oft Fotos herunter.

G

Separable verbs contain a **separable prefix**. In the present tense, this prefix 'snaps off' and goes to the end of the clause.
***an*rufen** (to call, phone)
Ich ***rufe*** *meine Freunde* ***an****.*
***herunter*laden** (to download)
Ich ***lade*** *Fotos* ***herunter****.*
***mit*bringen** (to bring along)
Ich ***bringe*** *mein Handy* ***mit****.*

4 Rewrite each sentence, putting the words into the correct order.

1 ruft oft seine an Freunde Er ....

2 bringen immer Sie den Computer mit ....

3 Fotos jede Woche herunter Wir laden ....

H 4 Ich viel aus gebe zweimal pro Woche Geld ....

H 5 sieht an jeden Tag Videos Sie sich ....

H 6 Serien schaue Ich an selten mir ....

H *sich anschauen* and *sich ansehen* appear in questions 5 and 6. You'll need to put the reflexive pronoun directly after the verb in each of these.

Start your sentence with the subject pronoun, which has a capital letter.

H 5 Translate these sentences into German using verbs from the box.

aufnehmen	mitbringen	anrufen
herunterladen	auswählen	hochladen

1 We upload text. ....

2 I call my friend. ....

3 They download photos. ....

4 What are you bringing with you? ....

5 You (informal, sg) normally record videos. ....

6 She chooses a strong password. ....

F 6 Translate these sentences into German.

1 I often stream music.

....

2 How often do you use your tablet?

....

3 I'm sending my number.

....

4 What messages do you write?

....

5 Every night I spend time online.

....

H 7 Translate this paragraph into English.

Mein Lieblingsgerät ist mein Smartphone. Ich kann eigentlich alles mit meinem Handy machen. Ich bin oft im Netz und mag besonders gern soziale Medien. Die Nachteile sind Cyberkriminalität und Mobbing. Man kann auch falsche Nachrichten finden. Aber es gibt viele Vorteile. Wenn ich Freizeit habe, dann plaudere ich mit Freunden.

....

....

....

....

....

....

3 Kommst du mit?

Asking questions

1 Match up the sentences with the clocks. Write the correct letter.

1 Es ist fünfundzwanzig vor fünf. ....

2 Es ist etwa zwölf Uhr. ....

3 Es ist zwanzig vor neun. ....

4 Es ist Viertel nach fünf. ....

5 Es ist Viertel vor zehn. ....

6 Es ist fast halb sieben. ....

7 Es ist fünfundzwanzig nach zwei. ....

8 Es ist halb elf. ....

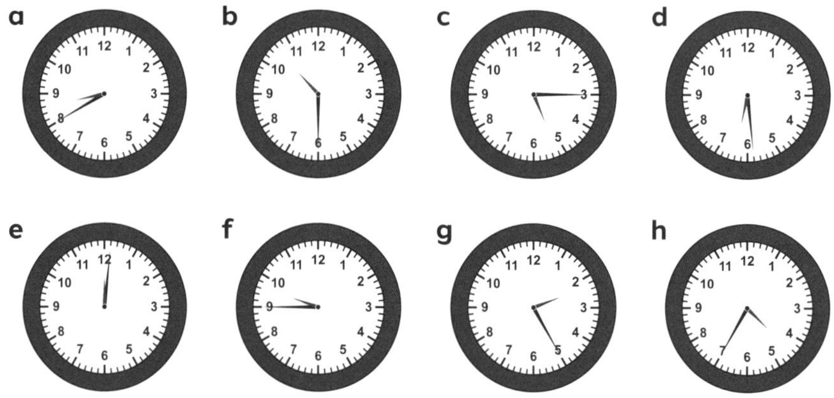

etwa	*about, approximately*
fast	*almost, nearly*

We use ***nach*** for times past the hour:
Es ist Viertel nach vier. It's a quarter past four.
We use ***vor*** for times to the hour:
Es ist Viertel vor vier. It's a quarter to four.
We say **half to** the next hour:
*Es ist **halb zehn**.* It's **half past nine**.

2 Complete the sentences by translating the word in brackets into German.

1 Möchtest du heute Abend ins .... (*cinema*) gehen?

2 Willst du morgen aufs .... (*concert*) gehen?

3 Können wir nach der Schule in ein .... (*café*) gehen?

4 Darfst du am Wochenende in ein .... (*restaurant*) gehen?

5 Wollt ihr ins .... (*theatre*) gehen?

H 6 Möchtet ihr eine .... (*exhibition*) im Museum sehen?

3 Complete each sentence by translating the phrase in brackets into German. Then put a tick or a cross in the box to indicate whether the person gives a positive or a negative response.

1 – (*Do you (informal, sg) want*) .... heute Abend ins Kino gehen?
– Ja, gerne. ☐

2 – (*Would you (informal, sg) like*) .... morgen aufs Konzert gehen?
– Es tut mir leid, ich darf nicht. ☐

3 – (*Do you (informal, sg) like*) .... Sendungen?
– Ich sehe lieber Filme. ☐

4 – Guten Tag! (*Would you (formal) like*) .... in einem Restaurant essen?
– Nein, danke. ☐

5 – (*Do you (formal) want*) .... einkaufen gehen?
– Vielleicht. ☐

H 6 – (*Are you (informal, sg) interested*) .... für klassische Musik?
– Ja, das höre ich oft zu Hause. Bis bald! ☐

G To ask yes/no questions, simply swap over the verb and the subject pronoun.
***Möchtest du** essen gehen?*
Would you like to go and eat?
***Willst du** etwas trinken?*
Do you want to drink something?

4 Complete each question using the correct question word or phrase.

1 .... kostet das? *How much does it cost?*

2 .... treffen wir uns? *Where are we meeting?*

3 .... kaufst du die Karten? *Why are you buying the tickets?*

4 .... gehst du nach Hause? *At what time are you going home?*

5 .... fährst du nach Hause? *How are you going home?*

H 6 .... tritt die Band auf? *When is the band appearing?*

G

You can also ask questions using **question words**:

Was? What?	*Warum?* Why?
Wo? Where?	*Welch-?* Which?
Wie? How?	*Wann?* When?
Wie viel? How much?, How many?	*Um wie viel Uhr?* At what time?
Wer? Who?	*Wie lange?* How long?

H 5 Separate out the words. Write out the questions and translate them into English on a separate sheet.

1 WannendetdasKonzert? ....

2 Kannichdichetwasfragen? ....

3 GibtesStudenten? ....

4 Istdaskostenlos? ....

5 TrittsieimKonzertauf? ....

6 UmwievielUhrfängtderFilman? ....

7 SieführendieGeschichteimSchultheaterauf. ....

Look out for the separable verbs here.

aufführen	*to perform*

F 6 Translate these sentences into English.

1 Ich interessiere mich für Schwimmen. ....

2 Möchtest du aufs Konzert gehen? ....

3 Vielleicht; wer spielt? ....

4 Wann beginnt der Film? ....

5 Das ist kostenlos für Studenten. ....

H 7 Translate this paragraph into German.

I would like to go to the cinema because I really like watching films. The comedy is playing at eight o'clock, so shall we meet early at half past seven? On Wednesday the cinema is free for students. I like going to the theatre but it is always very full and much too expensive.

Use the present tense of '(to) meet' for this.

....

....

....

....

4 Wie war der Film?

Using the imperfect and perfect tenses together

1 These adjectives are written in reverse order: write them out correctly. Then translate them into English.

1 treizilpmok ....
2 gnal ....
3 masgnal ....
4 gitsul ....
5 tkefrep ....
6 llenhcs ....
7 repus ....
8 hcsimok ....

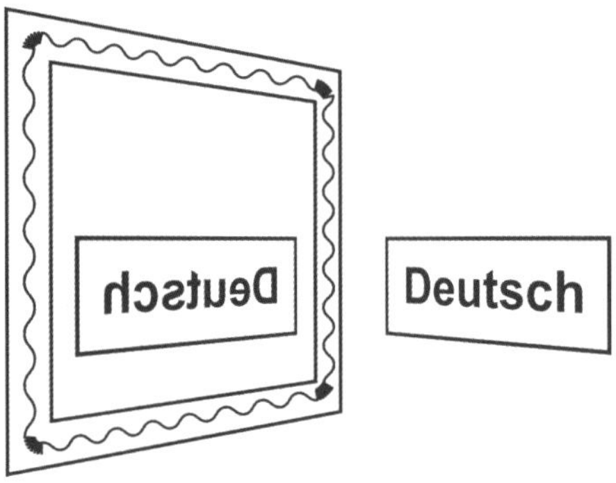

Try to learn as wide a variety of adjectives as possible. You can use intensifiers to strengthen or weaken your adjectives.
*Der Film ist **ganz** gut.* The film is **quite** good.
*Die Serie ist **sehr** langweilig.* The series is **very** boring.

2 Complete these sentences by translating the word(s) in brackets into German.

1 Ich finde .... (*adventure films*) ganz toll.
2 Ich mag .... (*comedies*), denn sie sind ziemlich super.
3 Ich denke, dass .... (*documentaries*) total perfekt sind.
4 Ich finde .... (*horror films*) besonders schnell.
5 Ich mag .... (*sports programmes*) nicht, weil sie komisch sind.
6 Ich finde .... (*series*) sehr lang.

You can use **denn** or **weil** to say 'because'. Remember that *weil* sends the verb to the end of the sentence, but *denn* does not.

3 Complete these perfect tense sentences with the past participle of the verb in brackets.

1 Ich bin ins Kino .... (*gehen*)
2 Ich habe einen Film im Fernsehen .... (*sehen*)
3 Ich habe die Serie toll .... (*finden*)
4 Ich habe im Restaurant .... essen)
5 Ich habe eine Komödie .... (*schreiben*)
6 Ich habe einen Krimi .... (*lesen*)

G To say what happened or what has happened, we use the **perfect tense**:
*Ich **habe** den Film **gesehen**.*
I **saw** / I **have seen** the film.
*Ich **habe** die Serie lustig **gefunden**.*
I **found** the series funny.
We can also use the **imperfect tense** when we're talking about past events:
*Es **hatte** viele lustige Momente.*
It **had** lots of funny moments.
*Es **war** langweilig.* It **was** boring.

4 Complete these sentences with an imperfect tense verb from the box.

1 Der Film .... toll.
2 Die Schauspieler .... super.

waren	fand	warst
sang	gab	hatte
war		

3 Ich .... viel Spaß.

4 Es .... viele Filme.

H 5 Ich .... die Serie langsam.

H 6 .... du zu Hause?

H 7 .... der Popstar gut?

> **G**
> The **perfect tense** is used in spoken German and more informal writing:
> *ich habe gesungen* I have sung / I sang
> *ich habe gefunden* I have found / I found
> The **imperfect tense** is used in written narrative texts, stories and reviews:
> H *ich sang* I sang
> H *ich fand* I found

H 5 Rewrite each sentence, replacing the underlined verb with the correct form of the perfect (P) or imperfect (I) tense as indicated in brackets.

1 Die Zuschauer <u>sind</u> sehr laut. (I) ....

2 Er <u>schreibt</u> eine Kritik. (P) ....

3 Es <u>gibt</u> vier Folgen. (I) ....

4 Wir <u>sehen</u> eine tolle Szene. (P) ....

5 Ich <u>finde</u> den Inhalt lustig. (I) ....

6 Der Schauspieler <u>kommt zu spät</u>. (P) ....

F 6 Translate these sentences into German.

1 I'm going to the cinema at the weekend. ....

2 I find comedies totally funny. ....

3 I like detective stories because they're fast. ....

4 The programme was particularly long. ....

5 I found the actors quite perfect. ....

H 7 Translate this paragraph into English.

Ich habe eine Kritik von diesem Krimi geschrieben. Ich fand ihn ziemlich langsam und er hat sehr spät geendet. Er hatte keine Spannung, aber ab und zu gab es ein bisschen zu viel Gewalt. Als Zuschauer sehe ich mir Dokumentarfilme nicht gern an, weil sie oft sehr kompliziert sind. Ich folge meinen Lieblingsschauspielern im Netz.

....

....

....

....

....

> **G**
> We can use the **present tense** with a **future time phrase** to talk about things we're **going to** do.
> *Morgen **sehe ich** fern.* Tomorrow **I'm going to watch** TV.
> *Am Wochenende **sehe ich** einen Actionfilm.*
> At the weekend **I'm going to watch** an action film.

> ★
> Use the glossary to look up any words that are unfamiliar, and try to learn them.

5 Hast du Pläne?

- Using the future tense to describe plans for the weekend
- Understanding the 'time – manner – place' rule

1 Translate the German time phrases using the English words in the box.

If there are words that you don't know, look them up in the glossary at the end of the module.

finally   afterwards   soon   firstly   then   after   finally

1 zuerst ....
2 dann ....
3 danach ....
4 endlich ....
H 5 nachdem ....
H 6 schließlich ....
H 7 bald ....

2 Draw lines to match up the sentence halves.

1 Ich werde allein Hausaufgaben
2 Er wird mit seinem Freund am Strand Fußball
3 Wir werden zu Hause Bücher
4 Sie wird mit ihrer Freundin Videos
5 Ich werde mit meiner Familie einkaufen
6 Wirst du im Park Rockmusik

a streamen.
b machen.
c lesen.
d hören?
e spielen.
f gehen.

3 Circle the correct part of *werden* to complete these sentences.

1 **Werde** / **Wirst** / **Werden** du allein Sport machen?
2 Er **werden** / **werde** / **wird** mit seinem Freund Popmusik hören.
3 Wir **wird** / **werde** / **werden** mit der Familie einen Film sehen.
4 Ich **wird** / **werde** / **werden** mein Handy benutzen.
5 Welche Aktivität **wirst** / **werden** / **wird** du machen?
6 Ich **wird** / **werde** / **werden** Fußball spielen.

G

We use the **future tense** to say what we **will** do. To form the future tense, use the present tense of ***werden*** and put the infinitive of another verb at the end of the clause.
Ich werde *im Kino einen Film sehen.*
I will see a film in the cinema.
Wirst du *in der Stadt einkaufen gehen?*
Will you go shopping in town?
Er wird *fernsehen.* **He will** watch TV.

4 Put the words into the correct order to make sentences. Remember the 'time – manner – place' rule.

1 Ich später zum Strand mit meiner Familie gehen werde
....
2 heute Nachmittag Er mit Familie der wird Videos streamen
....
3 mit Freundin meiner Ich morgen werde im Kino sehen Film einen
....
4 Samstag mit der werden der einkaufen Wir nächsten Familie in Stadt gehen
....

G

The usual correct word order for elements in a German sentence is:
1 time, **2 manner**, **3 place**.
So we need to say:
1 when we're doing the activity,
2 how we're doing the activity, and
3 where we're doing the activity.

5 allein wird Wochenende Sie am Hause Bücher zu lesen

....

H 6 werden mit Freunden in der Stadt ausgeben Wir viel Geld morgen früh

....

H 5 Complete the German translations.

1 Afterwards, I will go shopping in the shopping centre with my friends.

Danach .... *ich mit meinen* ....

einkaufen ....

2 Finally he will spend a lot of money.

Schließlich .... *er viel* ....

3 At the weekend she will do everything else in town with friends.

Sie .... *alles Andere mit Freundinnen*

in der Stadt ....

4 He will watch a film about heaven and Earth.

Er .... *über den Himmel und die Erde* ....

5 Last night he saw the start of the film and he will watch the rest this evening.

Gestern Abend hat er den .... *von dem Film* .... *und er wird den Rest*

.... *Abend sehen.*

6 We will stream videos at half past three with the family.

Wir .... *um halb vier* .... *Videos* ....

F 6 Translate these sentences into English.

1 Normalerweise gehe ich einkaufen.

....

2 Ich werde am Wochenende Videos streamen.

....

3 Er wird mit seinem Freund zum Strand gehen.

....

4 Wir werden später mit der Familie im Kino einen Film sehen.

....

5 Das wird toll sein. ....

H 7 Translate this paragraph into German on a separate sheet.

This afternoon I will spend lots of money because I will go shopping in town with my friends. Then we will go to the cinema and we will return late. That will be totally wonderful because I really like going to the cinema. What will you do?

The German for this word may need to go to the end of the sentence, depending on which word you choose for 'because'.

Glossary

bold = this word will appear in Higher exams only

		😕	🙂	😎
ab und zu	*now and again*			
Abend (m)	*evening*			
Abenteuer (nt)	*adventure*			
Aktivität (f)	*activity*			
allein	*alone*			
alles (Andere)	*everything (else)*			
also	*so, for that reason, therefore*			
am liebsten	*most rather, most preferred*			
anrufen	*(to) call, phone | calling, phoning*			
anschauen, sich anschauen	*(to) look at, watch | looking at, watching*			
ansehen, sich ansehen	*(to) watch, look at | watching, looking at*			
aufführen	*(to) perform | performing*			
aufnehmen	*(to) record | recording*			
auftreten	*(to) appear (on stage) | appearing (on stage)*			
ausgeben	*(to) spend (money), give out | spending (money), giving out*			
Ausstellung (f)	*exhibition*			
auswählen	*(to) choose, select | choosing, selecting*			
bald	*soon*			
Band (f)	*band, group*			
bekannt	*well-known, famous*			
benutzen	*(to) use | using*			
berühmt	*famous*			
besonders	*particularly*			
Bild (nt)	*picture*			

		😕	🙂	😎
bis bald	*see you soon*			
bisschen	*little, bit*			
chatten	*(to) chat online | chatting online*			
Cyberkriminalität (f)	*cybercrime*			
dann	*then*			
Daten (pl)	*data*			
denn	*because, for, since*			
digital	*digital*			
Ding (nt)	*thing*			
Dokumentarfilm (m)	*documentary*			
elektronisch	*electronic, electronically*			
enden	*(to) end, finish | ending, finishing*			
endlich	*finally, at last*			
Es tut mir leid	*I am sorry*			
etwa	*about, approximately*			
falsch	*wrong, wrongly, untrue*			
Familie (f)	*family*			
Fan (m)	*fan, supporter*			
fand	*(I/ she, he, it) found*			
fängt ... an	*(she, he, it, one) starts | is starting*			
fast	*almost, nearly*			
fernsehen	*(to) watch television, watch TV | watching television, watching TV*			
Fernsehen (nt); im Fernsehen	*television, TV; on television, on TV*			
Film (m)	*film*			
Folge (f)	*result, consequence*			
folgen	*(to) follow | following*			

fragen	*(to) ask | asking*
Freizeit (f)	*free time, leisure, theme (in 'theme park')*
früh	*early*
Gaming (nt)	*gaming*
ganz	*whole, all the, quite*
gar nicht	*not at all*
gehen	*(to) go, walk | going, walking*
Gerät (nt)	*appliance, piece of equipment*
gern, gerne	*gladly, (with a verb) like to*
Gewalt (f)	*violence, force*
Gruppe (f)	*group, gang*
Guten Tag	*hello*
halb	*half*
Handy (nt)	*mobile phone*
hatte	*(I / she, he, it, one) had | used to have | was having*
häufig	*frequent, frequently*
herunterladen	*(to) download | downloading*
Himmel (m)	*sky*
hören	*(to) hear, listen (to) | hearing, listening (to)*
Horror (m)	*horror*
immer	*always*
Inhalt (m)	*content, plot*
interessant	*interesting*
interessieren; sich interessieren für	*(to) interest | interesting; (to) be interested in | being interested in*
jed-(er, e, es)	*each, every (m, f, nt)*
kann	*(I) am / she, he, it, one is able to, can*
Karte (f)	*ticket, card, menu*
Kino (nt)	*cinema*
klassisch	*classic, classical, classically*
klingen	*(to) sound, ring | sounding, ringing*
kochen	*(to) cook | cooking*
komisch	*funny, funnily, strange, strangely*
Komödie (f)	*comedy*
kompliziert	*complicated, complicatedly*
können	*(to) be able to, can | being able to*
Konzert (nt)	*concert*
kostenlos	*free (of charge)*
Krimi (m)	*detective story, thriller*
Kritik (f)	*review, criticism*
lang, lange	*long, for a long time*
langsam	*slow, slowly*
Laptop (m) or (nt)	*laptop*
lesen	*(to) read | reading*
Liebe (f)	*love*
lieben	*(to) love | loving*
lieber	*more gladly, rather*
Lied (nt)	*song*
lustig	*funny, enjoyable*
malen	*(to) paint | painting*
manchmal	*sometimes*
Medien (pl)	*media*
mit (meinen) Freunden	*with (my) friends*
mitbringen	*(to) bring along | bringing along*
Mobbing (nt)	*bullying*

möchte	*(I / she, he, it, one) would like (to)*			
möchten	*(we / you (formal)/they) would like (to)*			
möchtest	*(you (sing informal)) would like (to)*			
möchtet	*(you (pl informal)) would like (to)*			
modern	*modern*			
modisch	*fashionable*			
mögen	*(to) like | liking*			
morgen	*tomorrow*			
morgen früh	*tomorrow morning*			
Nachricht (f)	*news, message*			
nächst-(er, e, es), nächste	*next (m, f, nt), (pl)*			
Nacht (f)	*night*			
Netz (nt)	*network*			
nie	*never*			
Nummer (f)	*number*			
online	*online*			
Passwort (nt)	*password*			
perfekt	*perfect, perfectly*			
Popmusik (f)	*pop music*			
produzieren	*(to) produce | producing*			
Programm (nt)	*channel*			
Publikum (nt)	*public, audience*			
Radfahren (nt)	*cycling*			
Rest (m); Reste (pl)	*rest, remainder; leftovers*			
Restaurant (nt)	*restaurant*			
Rockmusik (f), Rock (f)	*rock, rock music*			
Roman (m)	*novel*			
rufen	*(to) call, shout | calling, shouting*			
sang	*(I / she, he, it) sang*			
Sänger (m)	*singer*			
schauen	*(to) watch, look | watching, looking*			
Schauspieler (m)	*actor*			
schicken	*(to) send | sending*			
schließlich	*finally, after all*			
schnell	*quickly, quick, fast*			
schreiben	*(to) write | writing*			
sehen	*(to) see, watch, look | seeing, watching, looking*			
selten	*rare, rarely*			
Sendung (f)	*programme*			
Serie (f)	*series*			
singen	*(to) sing | singing*			
Smartphone (nt)	*smartphone*			
sozial	*social, socially*			
spannend	*exciting, excitingly, thrilling, tense*			
Spannung (f)	*suspense, tension*			
spät	*late*			
Spieler (m)	*player*			
Spielkonsole (f)	*games console*			
stammen (aus)	*(to) come from | coming from*			
Star (m)	*celebrity, star*			
Stil (m)	*style*			
Stimme (f)	*voice, vote*			
Stimmung (f)	*mood, atmosphere*			
streamen	*(to) stream | streaming*			
Streaming (nt)	*streaming*			
Student (m)	*student (university)*			
super	*super*			
Szene (f)	*scene*			
Tablet (nt)	*tablet*			
täglich	*every day, daily*			
Tanz (m)	*dance*			
toll	*great, terrific*			

Ton (m)	*sound, tone*
traurig	*sad, sadly*
(sich) treffen (mit)	*(to) meet | meeting*
türkisch	*Turkish*
üben	*(to) practise | practising*
überall	*everywhere*
Übung (f)	*practice, exercise*
Uhr (f)	*clock, watch, o'clock*
unbekannt	*unknown*
Verein (m)	*association, club*
verrückt	*mad, crazy*
Video (nt)	*video*
vielleicht	*perhaps*
Viertel (nt)	*quarter*
Virus (m)	*virus (computer)*
voll	*full, fully*
völlig	*completely*
wandern	*(to) hike | hiking*
werden	*(to) become | becoming | (we / you (formal) / they) become | are becoming | will (aux)*
will	*(I) want (to) | (she, he, it, one) wants (to)*
willst	*(you (sing informal)) want (to)*
wird	*(she, he, it, one) becomes | is becoming | will (aux)*
wirklich	*real, actual, really*
wirst	*(you (sing informal)) become | are becoming | will (aux)*
Wochenende (nt)	*weekend*
wöchentlich	*weekly, every week*
wollen	*(to) want (to) | wanting (to)*
wunderbar	*wonderful, wonderfully*
zeichnen	*(to) draw | drawing*
Zeitung (f)	*newspaper*
zu Hause	*at home; at my/ our house*
zurückkehren	*(to) return | returning*
Zuschauer (m)	*viewer, audience member*

Foundation translation revision

German to English

1 Rewrite each English translation, putting the English words into the correct order.

1 Ich höre nicht gern Popmusik. — *listening to I don't pop music like*

....

2 Dieses Lied ist sehr komisch. — *song This very is strange*

....

3 Ich bekomme immer viele Hausaufgaben. — *get I always a lot homework of*

....

4 Ich finde Deutsch sehr einfach. — *find German I very easy*

....

5 Letztes Wochenende war ich zu Hause. — *was I home at weekend Last*

....

2 Circle the mistake(s) in the English sentences. Then write out the correct English translations.

1 Ich spiele sehr gern Tennis. — *I don't like playing tennis.*

....

2 Dieses Konzert ist ganz gut. — *This film is quite good.*

....

3 Jede Woche bekommen wir eine Liste von den Schulregeln. — *Every day we get a list of the school rules.*

....

4 Ich finde Komödien gut, weil sie lustig sind. — *I find comedies great because they're exciting.*

....

5 Letzte Woche habe ich ein gelbes T-Shirt und eine weiße Hose getragen. — *Last weekend I wore a red t-shirt and black trousers.*

....

3 Translate these sentences into English on a separate sheet.

1 Ich höre sehr gern Rockmusik.

2 Dieses Lied ist sehr spannend und ziemlich schnell.

3 Jedes Jahr bekommen wir eine lange Liste von der Schule.

4 Ich finde Mathe schwierig, weil es kompliziert ist.

5 Letztes Wochenende habe ich einen schwarzen Hut, ein blaues Kleid und ein weißes Hemd getragen.

English to German

1 Colour one box from each column to translate each sentence (1–4) into German. Use a different colour for each sentence. Then write out your translations on a separate sheet.

Ich gehe	sehr gern	mit	Laptop
Letzte Woche	habe ich	in	ein Café.
Meine Lieblingstechnologie	gern	viele Sachen	gelernt.
Ich rede	ist	mein	meinen Freunden.

1 I like talking with my friends.

2 I really like going to a café.

3 My favourite technology is my laptop.

4 Last week I learned a lot of things.

2 Read the English paragraph. Number the German sentences in the correct order to translate it.

I like sports programmes. I really like listening to classical music because it's quiet. My favourite technology is my phone and it's new and blue. At school I wear jeans and a white t-shirt. Last summer I found history difficult.

1 Letzten Sommer habe ich Geschichte schwierig gefunden. ☐

2 Meine Lieblingstechnologie ist mein Handy und es ist neu und blau. ☐

3 Ich höre sehr gern klassische Musik, weil sie ruhig ist. ☐

4 Ich mag Sportsendungen. ☐

5 In der Schule trage ich eine Jeans und ein weißes T-Shirt. ☐

In exercise 3, there is a capital letter on the word you need to put at the start of your sentence. But remember that all nouns have a capital letter in German!

3 Rewrite each sentence, putting the words into the correct order.

1 Man die Hausaufgaben machen muss ....

2 Man seine Kleidung darf eigene tragen ....

3 mag kochen in Schule der mag nicht Ich ....

4 darf nicht Bibliothek in der reden Man ....

5 will Ich Hause nach gehen ....

4 Translate these sentences into German.

1 I like cooking with my family. ....

2 I really like listening to pop music because it's loud.

....

3 My favourite technology is my smartphone because it's necessary and important.

....

4 In school you aren't allowed to forget your homework.

....

5 Last week I spoke with my friends on my phone.

....

Higher translation revision

German to English

1 Complete the English translations.

1 Ich male jede Woche. — *I .... every ....*

2 Man kann mit Freunden plaudern. — *You can .... with ....*

3 Meine Lieblingssängerin singt Popmusik. — *My .... sings pop music.*

4 In der Schule mag ich die Regeln nicht, weil sie streng sind. — *At school I don't like the .... because they're ....*

5 Mobbing kann ein großes Problem sein. — *.............................. can be a .... problem.*

2 Choose the correct two English sentence halves (A–E), (a–e) to translate each German sentence (1–5). Write the correct letters.

1 Ich finde, dass die Ausstellung sehr interessant ist. ....

2 Ich denke, dass die Folgen sehr komisch sind. ....

3 Ich glaube, dass ich zu viel Geld für mein Handy ausgebe. ....

4 Wir finden, dass die Schuluniform nicht praktisch ist. ....

5 Wir denken, dass die Cyberkriminalität ein großes Problem ist. ....

A I believe that

B I think that

C We find that

D I find that

E We think that

a the episodes are very funny.

b the school uniform is not practical.

c cybercrime is a big problem.

d the exhibition is very interesting.

e I spend too much money on my mobile phone.

3 Translate this paragraph into English.

Ich zeichne wöchentlich, weil das ruhig ist. Ich finde, dass Musik sehr nützlich ist, denn man kann seine Probleme vergessen. Mein Lieblingssänger ist weltweit unbekannt, aber er singt schöne Lieder. Der Ton ist eigentlich sehr interessant. In der Schule mag ich die Schuluniform überhaupt nicht, weil sie unbequem ist.

....

....

....

....

....

....

English to German

1 Choose and colour a box from each column to translate the sentences (1–4) into German. Use a different colour for each sentence. Then write out your translations.

Ich singe	wichtiger Nachteil	sein Handy	Mobbing.
Heute Abend	darf man	in	einer Band.
Ein	gehe	ich in	nicht benutzen.
In der Schule	eigentlich	ist	ein Konzert.

1 I actually sing in a band. ....

2 One important disadvantage is bullying. ....

3 In school we aren't allowed to use our mobile phones. ....

4 This evening I'm going to a concert. ....

2 Translate the sentences (1–5) into German, using the first letter of each word to help you.

1 I perform songs with a band.

I	f	L	m	e	B	a

2 We are actually appearing this evening.

W	t	e	h	A	a

3 You can stay in contact with friends.

M	k	m	F	i	K	b

4 We are allowed to wear our own clothes.

M	d	s	e	K	t

5 The concert starts at eight o'clock.

D	K	f	u	a	U	a

3 Translate this paragraph into German.

I actually play in a group online with some friends. One important disadvantage of technology is cybercrime. At school we aren't allowed to chat in the library. It sounds very strange, but it's quite an important rule. This evening the film starts at seven o'clock, so do you want to come?

....

....

....

....

....

....

Kulturzone Feste in der deutschsprachigen Welt

Giving opinions and justifications

1 Draw lines to match up the German words with their English translations.

1 das Ausland
2 das Geschenk
3 der Markt
4 die Schokolade
H 5 das Fest
H 6 die Blume
H 7 das Ereignis

a festival, holiday
b flower
c market
d event
e present
f chocolate
g foreign countries, abroad

2 Fill in the missing words in German.

1 Die Wagen im Karneval sind laut und ....(*colourful*).
2 Der Karneval hat in Deutschland eine lange ....(*tradition*).
H 3 In Österreich gibt es ein Sportfest in der ....(*nature*).
H 4 Am fünften Dezember ....(*fill*) die Eltern die Schuhe der Kinder mit Schokolade.
H 5 Das Oktoberfest ist ein ganz besonderes ....(*festival*).

> Use a range of structures to give your opinion and justify it:
> ***Ich finde*** *das Eisfest toll,* ***weil*** *ich die Natur mag.*
> **I find** the ice festival great **because** I like nature.
> ***Meiner Meinung nach*** *ist das Lauffest schön,* ***weil*** *ich ein großer Sportfan bin.*
> **In my opinion**, the running festival is great **because** I'm a big sports fan.
> *Karneval* ***interessiert mich (nicht), weil*** *es (zu) viele Leute gibt.*
> I'm **(not) interested in** carnival **because** there are (too) many people.

3 Draw lines to match up the sentence halves.

1 Ich finde Karneval toll, weil
2 Meiner Meinung nach ist der Markt teuer, weil
3 Das Straßenkunstfest interessiert mich, weil es
4 Ich finde das Musikfest langweilig, weil
5 Meiner Meinung nach ist das Radsportfest wunderbar, weil

a ich Radfahren mag.
b das Essen zu viel kostet.
c die Wagen so schön und bunt sind.
d ich Musik nicht mag.
e viele einzelne Künstler dort gibt.

4 Rewrite each sentence, putting the word groups into the correct order.

1 den Markt schlecht, / es zu viele Leute gibt. / Ich finde / weil

....

2 weil / ist Karneval toll, / Meiner Meinung nach / die Leute viel lachen.

....

3 ist das Oktoberfest / Meiner Meinung / ich gern tanze. / nach / schön, weil

....

H 4 schöne Blumen sieht. / man hier viele / weil / das Blumenfest / Ich finde / toll,

....

H 5 weil mir Schwimmen / Winterschwimmen interessiert / keinen Spaß macht. / mich nicht,

....

H 5 Separate out the words and write out the German sentences. Remember to add capital letters to the nouns and a comma before *weil*.

1 Ichfindedenweihnachtsmarktschlechtweileseinemengeleutegibt.

....

2 Meinermeinungnachistdieveranstaltunginteressantweilmirkunstgutgefällt.

....

3 Dasoktoberfestinteressiertmichnichtweildiegetränkezuteuersind.

....

4 Dugefällstmirintraditionellerkleidungweilichbuntekleidungmag.

....

F 6 Translate these sentences into English.

1 Ich finde den Markt toll. ....

2 Karneval ist wunderbar, weil es viel bunte Kleidung gibt.

....

3 Viele Menschen schwimmen im kalten Wasser.

....

4 Wir finden die Party langweilig, weil sie sehr laut ist.

....

5 Ich habe traditionelles Essen auf dem Oktoberfest gegessen.

....

H 7 Translate this paragraph into German.

In spring the street art festival takes place. The festival lasts two days and you can see here artists from all over the world. There is a lot of music, delicious food and great drinks. I find the festival fantastic because you laugh and dance a lot. Do you also want to take part next year?

....

....

....

....

....

1 Wie ist deine Familie?

Using possessive adjectives • Using relative pronouns

1 Match up the German words with their English translations. Write the correct letter.

1 Kaninchen ....
2 Bruder ....
3 Eltern ....
4 Großeltern ....
5 Tante ....
H 6 Verwandte ....
H 7 Zwilling ....

a relative	**e** rabbit
b parents	**f** twin
c aunt	**g** brother
d grandparents	

2 Complete each sentence using a word from the box.

1 Meine Großmutter ist nicht groß und trägt eine ....
2 Meine Mutter hat kurze weiße .... und ist ziemlich klein.
3 Ich habe auch zwei ältere ....
4 Mein Fisch .... Steven und ist total sportlich.
5 Unsere Katze ist immer freundlich und .... oft.
6 Meine Schwester, die du gut ...., ist nie böse.
H 7 Mein Zwillingsbruder ist mir nicht ähnlich. Er ist ganz ....
H 8 Mein Großvater hat viele gute ....

lächelt
Brille
Eigenschaften
heißt
kennst
anders
Brüder
Haare

3 Complete this text with the correct forms of the possessive adjective (*mein*, *meine* or *meinen*).

1 .... Name ist Erik und ich wohne jetzt mit meiner Halbschwester zusammen in Wien. **2** .... Halbschwester heißt Susanne und ist sehr freundlich. **3** .... Brüder Tim und Anton sind noch klein und wohnen bei unseren Eltern in Salzburg. **4** .... Papa heißt Martin und er ist sehr freundlich. **5** .... Mama heißt Luise und sie ist immer total lieb! Ich liebe **6** .... Eltern sehr! Wir haben auch Tiere. Ich mag **7** .... Katze sehr! Sie heißt Minka und schläft viel. Ich liebe auch **8** .... Fisch, aber er ist oft traurig. Aber **9** .... Hund mag ich eigentlich nicht. Er ist oft böse!

G

Possessive adjectives follow the same pattern as the indefinite article *ein*. Only the masculine form changes in the accusative. Remember that adjective endings need to agree with the noun they are describing.

	nominative (subject)	**accusative (object)**
masculine	mein (groß**er**) Bruder	mein**en** (groß**en**) Bruder
feminine	mein**e** (traurig**e**) Tante	mein**e** (traurig**e**) Tante
neuter	mein (grau**es**) Kaninchen	mein (grau**es**) Kaninchen
plural	mein**e** (lieb**en**) Verwandten	mein**e** (lieb**en**) Verwandten

These possessive adjectives also follow the same pattern:
dein (your – familiar, sg), ***sein*** (his), ***ihr*** (her),
unser (our), ***eu(e)r*** (your – familiar, pl),
Ihr (your – formal), ***ihr*** (their)

4 Complete these sentences with the correct possessive adjective.

1 .... (*her*) Onkel Hans wohnt in der Schweiz.
2 Karli, ... (*your, informal*) Katze hat einen schlechten Charakter!

3 Frau Müller, wo leben .... (*your, formal*) Eltern?

H 4 .... (*his*) Tante Lisa trägt eine schmale Brille.

H 5 Lena und Tim, ... (*your, informal pl*) Zwillinge sind sehr süß.

H 6 Tom besucht .... (*our*) Großvater wenigstens zweimal im Jahr.

G

Relative pronouns (who, which) refer back to someone or something. They send the verb to the end of the clause.
Relative pronouns must be used in the same case as the noun to which they refer.
Subject (nom): ***Dein großer Bruder*, *der*** *Theo heißt, ist sehr lustig.* (Here, **der** (referring back to ***dein großer Bruder***) is the subject of the relative clause.)
H **Object (acc):** ***Dein großer Bruder*, *den*** *ich sehr mag, ist lustig.* (Here, *ich* is the subject and **den** is the object of the relative clause.)

	German	English
masc.	Mein (großer) Bruder, ***der*** ...	My (big) brother, **who** ...
fem.	Meine (traurige) Tante, ***die*** ...	My (sad) aunt, **who** ...
neuter	Mein (graues) Kaninchen, ***das*** ...	My (grey) rabbit, **which** ...
plural	Meine (lieben) Verwandten, ***die*** ...	My (dear) relatives, **who** ...

5 Circle the correct relative pronoun to complete each sentence.

1 Unsere Geschwister, **der / die / das** nicht auf dem Foto sind, wohnen in Berlin.

2 Euer Fisch, **der / das / den** sehr allein ist, ist manchmal traurig.

H 3 Sein Onkel, **der / die / den** ich nicht kenne, interessiert sich für die Natur.

H 4 Ihre Tante, **die / das / den** ich sehr mag, hat nie geheiratet.

H 5 Eure Großmutter, **der / die / das** keine Brille trägt, hat blaue Augen.

H 6 Dein Bruder, **der / das / den** viele gute Eigenschaften hat, ist immer glücklich.

F **6 Translate these sentences into German.**

1 My sister is quite small. ....

2 I find my dog, who is called Felix, totally funny!

....

3 Do you know my stepbrother who lives in London?

....

4 Her rabbit, which is black and white, is nine years old.

....

5 His friend was very friendly. ....

H **7 Translate this paragraph into English on a separate sheet.**

Mein Name ist Lukas und auf dem Foto sieht man meine Verwandten. Wir waren auf dem Blumenfest. Mein Onkel und meine Tante, die in Wien wohnen, heißen Martin und Frida. Meine Stiefmutter, die immer lächelt, heißt Linda. Mein Vater, den ich total liebe, hat kurze rote Haare. Und unser Fisch, der Finn heißt, ist völlig locker.

2 Wer bist du?

Using pronouns and possessive adjectives in the dative

1 Fill in the missing letters.

1 Fre_n_in
2 H_l_br_der
3 To_ht_r
4 On_el
5 T_n_e
H 6 B_zie_ung
H 7 V_rh_ltn_s

2 Underline the adjective in each sentence and translate it into English.

1 Wer ist ganz sportlich? ....
2 Mein Sohn ist oft gestresst. ....
3 Unsere Töchter sind sehr fleißig. ....
H 4 Unsere Oma ist total nett. ....
H 5 Unser Opa ist wirklich streng. ....
H 6 Meine Stiefschwester ist ziemlich unabhängig. ....

G

Some prepositions, like *mit* (with), are always followed by **dative** pronouns or possessive adjectives.
Ich verstehe mich (nicht) gut ***mit*** *...*
I (don't) get on well **with** ...

masculine	mein**em** Bruder	**ihm**
feminine	mein**er** Tante	**ihr**
neuter	mein**em** Kind	**ihm**
plural	mein**en** Eltern	H **ihnen**

3 Circle the correct dative possessive adjective to complete each sentence.

1 Ich verstehe mich gut mit **meiner** / **meinem** / **meinen** Sohn.
2 Verstehst du dich gut mit **deiner** / **deinem** / **deinen** Eltern?
3 Ja, ich verstehe mich gut mit **meiner** / **meinem** / **meinen** Kind.
4 Ich verstehe mich nicht gut mit **meiner** / **meinem** / **meinen** Stiefmutter.
5 Aber ich verstehe mich sehr gut mit **meiner** / **meinem** / **meinen** Tante.

4 Complete these sentences with the correct dative pronoun.

1 Meine Stiefschwester ist sehr freundlich und ich verstehe mich gut mit ....
2 Dein Bruder ist sehr nett. Verstehst du dich gut mit ....?
3 Ich glaube fest an ihn und ich verstehe mich sehr gut mit ....
H 4 Meine Großeltern sind ehrlich, aber zu ernst, und ich verstehe mich nicht so gut mit ....
H 5 Meine Zwillingsschwester und ich sind so unterschiedlich und ich verstehe mich nicht gut mit ....

H 5 Complete these sentences with the correct pronoun from the box to replace the underlined words.

uns ihm ihr dir ihnen ihm euch

1 Ich spiele mit meinem Kaninchen.

Ich spiele mit ....

2 Ich war zusammen mit meinen Freundinnen auf dem Fest.

Ich war zusammen mit .... auf dem Fest.

3 Ich verstehe mich gut mit meinem Opa.

Ich verstehe mich gut mit ....

4 Kommst du mit Daniel und mir ins Kino?

Kommst du mit .... ins Kino?

5 Ich fahre mit dir und deiner Tante nach Berlin.

Ich fahre mit .... nach Berlin.

6 Ich gehe mit meiner Freundin spazieren.

Ich gehe mit .... spazieren.

G

nominative	dative
ich	mir
du	dir
er	ihm
sie	ihr
es	ihm
wir	H uns
ihr	H euch
Sie	Ihnen
sie	H ihnen

F 6 Translate these sentences into English.

1 Ich verstehe mich sehr gut mit meinem Stiefvater.

....

2 Mein Bruder ist immer so gestresst und fast nie glücklich.

....

3 Du bist sehr aktiv und ich spiele oft Fußball mit dir.

....

4 Du hast dieselben Interessen und verstehst dich gut mit mir.

....

5 Frau Müller, Sie sind so nett und ich möchte gern mit Ihnen essen gehen.

....

H 7 Translate this paragraph into German.

I have a very good relationship with my stepmother because she is really totally relaxed. But my father – I don't get on so well with him because he is always too stressed. My brothers, the twins, are sometimes quite loud, but that is normal. We all get on really well with them.

....

....

....

....

....

3 Wen respektierst du?

- Using two time frames together: past and present
- Recognising feminine nouns

1 Unjumble the letters to rewrite the words correctly.

1 liuatQät ....

2 ertiewlvn ....

3 eeruhindnBg ....

4 isssmRaus ....

5 eisSmusx ....

H 6 ndeiterMih ....

H 7 toeIngnrati ....

2 Underline the noun(s) in each sentence and translate them into English on a separate sheet.

1 Die Situation ist seltsam und wir müssen etwas ändern.

2 Sie hat viel für die Rechte von Menschen gemacht, zum Beispiel für die, die schwul, lesbisch oder nicht-binär sind.

H 3 Oft sind solche Probleme immer noch ein Teil ihres Lebens.

H 4 Der Kampf für die Opfer von Mobbing ist total wichtig.

H 5 Er ist ein toller Typ und ein Vorbild für die Jugend, denn er kämpft gegen die religiöse Diskriminierung in unserer Gesellschaft.

Try to work out the meaning of the sentences. If you come across words you don't yet know, look them up in the glossary at the end of the module.

G

Use the present and past tenses alongside each other to add interest and complexity to your German.

*Sie **ist** Aktivistin und **hat** immer viel gegen Sexismus **gemacht**.*

She **is** an activist and **has** always **done** a lot against sexism.

G

Remember:

- In the **perfect tense**, verbs involving **movement** or a **change of state** take ***sein***.
- The **past participle for regular verbs** is formed by adding ***ge-*** to the start and **-t** to the end of the verb stem.
- Some irregular verbs add -***en*** instead of **-t**, and others have a vowel change or are completely irregular.

3 Write the correct tense (past (P) or present (Pr)) for each sentence. Then translate the sentences into English.

1 Ich finde, wir müssen einander respektieren. [ ]

....

2 Er erzählt wie für ihn Sexismus oft ein Problem ist. [ ]

....

3 Wir haben früher viele Probleme mit Diskriminierung gehabt. [ ]

....

4 Er hat seine Position gewechselt, weil er Probleme mit Rassismus bei der Arbeit hatte. [ ]

....

H 5 Sie hat viel gegen Rassismus gemacht. [ ]

....

H 6 Ich finde, dass er einen sehr positiven Einfluss hat und dass ihm viele Menschen vertrauen. [ ]

....

H **7** Wir müssen die Gesetze gegen Rassismus in alle Sprachen übersetzen. ☐

....

4 Complete these sentences with the correct tense of the verbs in brackets.

1 Emily .... alle Leute und .... vielen Menschen. (*respektieren* – present, *helfen* – present)

2 Ich .... eine Behinderung, aber das ist mir egal, denn ich .... mein Leben. (*haben* – present, *lieben* – present)

3 Paula .... bei einer Zeitung und hat ein Interview mit einem lesbischen Paar .... (*arbeiten* – present, *machen* – perfect)

H **4** Er .... in der Minderheit und .... deshalb schon oft Mobbing .... (*sein* – present, *erleben* – perfect)

H **5** Damals ist mein Bruder heterosexuell ...., aber heute .... er bisexuell. (*sein* – perfect, *sein* – present)

H **6** Manche Leute .... schon oft Rassismus .... und .... sich nun in Deutschland nicht .... (*erleben* – perfect, *wohlfühlen* – present)

wohlfühlen is a separable verb.

H **5 Underline the feminine nouns and translate them into English on a separate sheet.**

1 Ich finde, dass es viele Unterschiede zwischen den Menschen gibt, aber dass wir alle positive Qualitäten haben.

2 Er unterstützt viele Opfer von Rassismus und andere Minderheiten.

3 Sie ist behindert und hat viel Mobbing in der Gesellschaft erlebt.

4 62 Jahre ist kein hohes Alter, aber er hat auf der Arbeit schon oft Diskriminierung erfahren.

5 Ich finde, dass in Wirklichkeit die Situation jetzt schon viel besser für meine Familie ist.

Nouns with these endings are usually feminine: *-heit, -keit, -ung, -tät, -schaft, -ion, -ie*.
Can you spot the feminine nouns in exercise 1?

F **6 Translate these sentences into German on a separate sheet.**

1 My family has no problems with racism.

2 I respect all cultures and religions.

3 Freedom is essential to me.

4 I think that the rights of people with disabilities are very important.

5 My uncle is gay and has always had problems with discrimination.

Remember that the conjunction ***dass*** is used to link two clauses. Like *weil*, it sends the verb to the end of the sentence.
*Ich finde, **dass** sie viele positive Qualitäten hat.*
I think **that** she has many positive qualities.

H **7 Translate this paragraph into English on a separate sheet.**

Ich finde, dass er für alle Menschen ein wunderbares Vorbild ist. Er hat immer gegen Rassismus gekämpft. Leider erleben manche Menschen immer noch viel Diskriminierung, was mich sehr aufregt. Auch Sexismus ist ein großes Problem. Ich finde, dass es wirklich wichtig ist, Unterschiede und andere Kulturen und Religionen zu akzeptieren.

4 Wir haben gefeiert!

Practising word order

1 Translate these words into English.

1 das Feuerwerk ....

2 der Geburtstag ....

3 die Ferien ....

4 der Anfang ....

5 der Morgen ....

6 der Freizeitpark ....

2 Complete these sentences by translating the verbs in brackets into German.

1 Am Wochenende bin ich mit meiner Freundin ins Kino .... (*gone*).

2 Nach den Prüfungen haben wir .... (*celebrated*)

3 Am Anfang ...., wie üblich, ein großes Feuerwerk. (*there was*)

4 An Silvester haben wir viel Spaß .... (*had*)

5 Er hat uns etwas über seine Ferien .... (*told*)

3 Rewrite these sentences, adding the adverbial phrase in brackets in the correct position.

1 Wir waren auf dem Fest. (*am Wochenende*)

....

2 Ich bin am Nachmittag auf den Markt gegangen. (*mit meinem Bruder*)

....

....

3 Ich habe Nico am Mittwoch gesehen. (*im Restaurant*)

....

....

4 Ich habe mit meiner Familie gefeiert. (*bei meinen Großeltern*)

....

....

> **G**
> Remember the word order rule: **time** (when) – ***manner*** (how) – **place** (where):
> *Ich habe* **letztes Jahr** *Karneval* ***mit meinen Freunden*** **in Köln** *gefeiert.*
> Remember that the **verb** always stays in second position:
> *Im Oktober* ***habe*** *ich meinen Geburtstag mit meiner Familie zu Hause gefeiert.*
> **H** *Am Sonntag* ***habe*** *ich Peter nochmal alles Gute zum Geburtstag im Restaurant gewünscht.*

> Remember that the place comes last, just before the past participle.

4 Rewrite these sentences using the correct word order. Keep the underlined word group first each time.

1 Wir haben / meinen Geburtstag / gefeiert / im Freizeitpark / letzten Freitag

....

2 Nach den Prüfungen / mit meiner Freundin / habe ich / gegessen / am Strand

....

3 Anja und Peter / gefahren / mit dem Zug / zum Oktoberfest / sind letzte Woche

....

H **4** Lise ist / mit ihrem Freund / auf dem Karneval / gewesen / neulich

....

bestanden is the past participle of *bestehen*.

H **5** Ich habe / meine Prüfung bestanden und habe deshalb / im Stadtzentrum / gefeiert / am Freitag / mit meinen Großeltern

....

....

H 5 Write sentences to answer these questions, using correct word order and the phrases in brackets.

Wann, mit wem und wo hast du ...

1 ... ein Musikfest besucht? (*im Dorf, am Samstag, mit meinen Geschwistern*)

....

2 ... deinen Geburtstag gefeiert? (*mit meinem Bruder, am Strand, im August*)

....

3 ... eine Party organisiert? (*im Restaurant, mit meinem Onkel, am Freitag*)

....

4 ... ein großes Feuerwerk gesehen? (*im Stadtzentrum, am Wochenende, mit meiner Freundin*)

....

F 6 Translate these sentences into English.

1 Ich feiere am 31. Dezember mit meinen Schwestern Silvester.

....

2 Meine Mutter organisiert im Juni eine Geburtstagsparty im Garten.

....

3 Ich habe in den Ferien mit meinen Eltern einen tollen Film im Kino gesehen.

....

4 Ich habe mit meiner Familie zu Hause viel gegessen und getrunken.

....

5 Wir haben am Karneval in Köln getanzt, gelacht und viele nette Leute kennengelernt.

....

H 7 Translate this paragraph into German on a separate sheet.

Last month, I went with my friends to the famous Oktoberfest. The festival takes place annually in Munich. I really enjoyed the festival and the atmosphere was fantastic! We had a lot of fun and laughed, danced and sang the whole day. We also ate a lot and met nice people.

5 Partyzeit!

- Using two time frames together: past and future
- Using *in* + accusative or dative

1 Translate these words into German. Include the definite article (*der*, *die* or *das*).

1 cake ....
2 cinema ....
3 classroom ....
4 swimming pool ....
5 city centre ....

2 Complete each sentence using a verb from the box.

hören lesen
gefeiert gelacht
gekannt sehen
gemacht

1 Am Mittwoch habe ich mit meinen Freunden im Garten eine Party ....
2 Wir haben den Anfang der Ferien ....
3 Wir haben viel gegessen, getanzt und ....
4 In den Ferien werde ich viel schlafen und Musik ....
5 Ich werde auch ins Kino gehen und Filme ....
6 Natürlich werde ich in den Ferien auch Bücher ....
H 7 Letzten Sommer habe ich deine neuen Freunde schon ....

G

To add interest and complexity to your German, use the past and future tenses in your work.

Past	Future
Ich **habe** eine Geburtstagsparty **geplant**.	Ich **werde** eine Geburtstagsparty **planen**.
Das **hat** viel Spaß **gemacht**.	Das **wird** viel Spaß **machen**.
Auf der Party **haben** wir viel Kuchen **gegessen**.	Auf der Party **werden** wir viel Kuchen **essen**.
H Sie **hat** im Schwimmbad **stattgefunden**.	H Sie **wird** im Schwimmbad **stattfinden**.

3 Circle the correct form of the verb to complete each sentence.

1 Letztes Wochenende **hat** / **wird** meine Tante geheiratet.
2 Am Montag **haben** / **werden** wir den Anfang der Ferien feiern.
3 Am Sonntag **habe** / **werde** ich mit meinen Eltern zu Hause essen.
4 Wir **haben** / **werden** ein Spiel gespielt, viel gelacht und getrunken.
5 Nächsten Monat **habe** / **werde** ich mit meiner Familie nach Berlin fahren.

To help you decide which tense is needed, look at the time expressions, and whether a past participle or infinitive is used at the end of the sentence.

4 Rewrite these perfect tense sentences in the future tense.

1 Ich habe am Wochenende eine Geburtstagsparty gemacht.

....

2 Ich habe viele schöne Geschenke bekommen.

....

H 3 Ich habe dich eingeladen und meinen Kuchen mit dir geteilt.

....

H 4 Meine Oma hat mich mit einem leckeren Kuchen überrascht.

....

H 5 Mein Bruder hat sich nicht an meinen Geburtstag erinnert.

....

G

Some prepositions such as ***in*** can be followed by either the **accusative** case (indicating **movement**) or the **dative** case (indicating **position**).

		masculine	**feminine**	**neuter**	**plural**
accusative (movement)	ich gehe **in**	**den** Garten	**die** Schule	**das** Restaurant	**die** Geschäfte
dative (position)	ich bin **in**	**dem** Garten	**der** Schule	**dem** Restaurant	**den** Geschäften

in dem is often abbreviated to ***im***. ***in das*** is often abbreviated to ***ins***.

5 Complete these sentences with the correct form of the definite article.

1 Am Wochenende werde ich mit Freunden in .... Freizeitpark (*m*) gehen.

2 Im Sommer sind wir oft in .... Schwimmbad (*nt*) gegangen.

3 Am Samstag werde ich in .... Stadtmitte (*f*) gehen und einen Kuchen kaufen.

4 In .... Restaurants (*pl*) haben viele Leute ihren Geburtstag gefeiert.

5 Wir waren in .... Schule (*f*) und haben den Anfang der Ferien gefeiert.

6 Die Geschwister haben den Tennisspiel in .... Park gewonnen.

H 7 In .... Klassenzimmer (*nt*) gab es viele Geschenke.

F **6 Translate these sentences into German.**

1 We eat very well at home. ....

2 Last week I celebrated my birthday at the swimming pool.

....

3 On Wednesday I will go to the restaurant.

....

4 On Friday we went to the cinema but on Saturday we will go into town.

....

5 Yesterday I learned maths but in the holidays I will be in the park a lot.

....

H **7 Translate this paragraph into English on a separate sheet.**

Im Dezember habe ich eine große Geburtstagsparty für meine Halbschwester organsiert. Sie war total überrascht, weil ich ihr vorher nichts gesagt habe. Das Ereignis hat im Haus stattgefunden. Im Juli werde ich eine Party für meinen Onkel machen. Die Feier wird im Garten sein, weil sie im Sommer ist.

Glossary

bold = this word will appear in Higher exams only

(aus)füllen	*(to) fill (in) / filling (in)*
ähnlich	*similar*
aktiv	*active, actively*
alles Gute	*all the best*
älter	*older*
Alter (nt)	*age*
ander	*other*
ändern	*(to) change, alter / changing, altering*
anders	*different, differently*
Anfang (m); am Anfang	*start, beginning; in the beginning*
auch	*also, too, as well*
aufregen	*(to) excite, upset, annoy / exciting, upsetting, annoying*
Ausland (nt); im / ins Ausland	*foreign countries; abroad*
behindert	*disabled*
Behinderung (f)	*disability*
Beispiel (nt); zum Beispiel, z.B.	*example; for example, e.g.*
besonder	*special*
besser	*better*
bestehen	*(to) pass (an exam) / passing (an exam)*
Beziehung (f)	*relationship*
bisexuell	*bisexual*
bist	*(you (sing informal)) are / are being*
Blume (f)	*flower*
böse	*angry, angrily, bad*
Brille (f)	*glasses*
Bruder (m)	*brother*
Brüder (pl)	*brothers*
bunt	*colourful*
Charakter (m)	*character*
damals	*then, at that time*
das	*which, who, this, these, that (nt)*
dein	*your (m, nt)*
deine	*your (f, pl)*
der	*which, who (m)*
deshalb	*therefore*
dich	*you (obj) / yourself (reflex)*
die	*which, who (f, pl)*
dir	*(to/for) you (indirect obj)*
Diskriminierung (f)	*discrimination*
ehrlich	*honest, honestly*
Eigenschaft (f)	*characteristic, quality*
eigentlich nicht	*not really*
einander	*each other, one another*
Einfluss (m)	*influence*
(aux) ... eingeladen	*invited / (have, has) invited*
einladen	*(to) invite / inviting*
einzel	*single, individual, only*
Eltern (pl)	*parents*
Ereignis (nt)	*event*
erfahren	*(to) experience, find out / experiencing, finding out*
erinnern; sich erinnern an	*(to) remind / reminding; (to) remember / remembering*
erleben	*(to) experience / experiencing*

ernst	*serious, seriously, earnest, earnestly*
erzählen	*(to) tell | telling*
Es ist mir egal	*I don't mind, I'm not bothered*
es (...) gab	*there was / were / used to be*
euch	***(to) you (pl informal) (obj)*** */ yourselves (informal) (reflex) / each other (informal) (reciprocal)*
euer	*your (informal, pl) (m, nt)*
eure	*your (informal, pl) (f, pl)*
feiern	*(to) celebrate | celebrating*
Ferien (pl)	*holidays, vacation*
fest	*firm, firmly, solid*
Fest (nt)	*festival, holiday, fair, party*
Feuer (nt)	*fire*
Fisch (m)	*fish*
fleißig	*hard-working*
Freund (m)	*friend, ally, boyfriend*
Freundin (f)	*friend, ally, girlfriend*
freundlich	*friendly, nice, kind, kindly*
Geburtstag (m)	*birthday*
gefallen	*(to) please | pleasing*
gefällst	*(you (sing informal)) please | are pleasing*
(aux) ... gegangen	*went, walked / (have, has) gone, walked*
(aux) ... gegessen	*ate / (have, has) eaten*

(aux) ... gekannt	*knew / (have, has) known*
(aux) ... gewonnen	*won / (have, has) won*
Geschenk (nt)	*present, gift*
Gesellschaft (f)	*society, company*
Gesetz (nt)	*law*
gestresst	*stressed*
Getränk (nt)	*drink*
groß	*big, tall, great*
Großeltern (pl)	*grandparents*
Großmutter (f)/ Grossmutter	*grandmother*
Großvater (m)/ Grossvater	*grandfather*
Haar (nt)	*hair*
Halb- (prefix)	*half (e.g. brother)*
heißt	*(you (sing informal)) are called / (she, he, it, one) is called*
hetero(sexuell)	*straight*
hier	*here*
Hund (m)	*dog*
ihm	*(to/for) him (indirect obj), (to/for) it (m, nt) (indirect obj)*
ihn	*him (obj), it (m) (obj)*
Ihnen	*(to/for) you (formal, indirect obj)*
ihnen	*(to/for) them*
Ihr	*your (formal) (m, nt)*
ihre	*her, its, their (f, pl)*
immer noch	*still*
Integration (f)	*integration*
Interesse (nt)	*interest*
Interview (nt)	*interview*
jährlich	*yearly, annual*
jetzt	*now*

		😐	🙂	😎
Jugend (f)	*youth, young people*			
Kampf (m)	*fight, struggle*			
kämpfen	*(to) fight, struggle | fighting, struggling*			
Kaninchen (nt)	*rabbit*			
Katze (f)	*cat*			
kennen	*(to) know | knowing*			
klein	*small*			
Kuchen (m)	*cake*			
Künstler (m)	*artist*			
kurz	*short, brief*			
lächeln	*(to) smile | smiling*			
lachen	*(to) laugh | laughing*			
lesbisch	*lesbian*			
Leute (pl)	*people*			
lieb	*kind, dear*			
locker	*loose (clothing), relaxed*			
Mama (f)	*mum*			
manche	*some*			
Markt (m)	*market*			
meiner Meinung nach	*in my opinion*			
Meinung (f)	*opinion*			
Menge (f)	*quantity, amount, crowd*			
Mensch (m)	*person, human being*			
mich	*me (obj) / myself (reflex)*			
Minderheit (f)	*minority*			
mir	*(to/for) me (indirect obj)*			
Morgen (m)	*morning*			
Mutter (f)	*mother*			
Name (m)	*name*			
Natur (f)	*nature, countryside*			

		😐	🙂	😎
nett	*nice, kind, pretty*			
neulich	*recently, the other day*			
nochmal	*again*			
normal	*normal*			
nun	*now*			
Oma (f)	*grandma, granny*			
Onkel (m)	*uncle*			
Opa (m)	*grandad*			
Opfer (nt)	*victim*			
organisieren	*(to) organise | organising*			
Paar (nt)	*pair, couple*			
Papa (m)	*dad*			
Party (f)	*party*			
Position (f)	*job, position*			
Problem (nt)	*problem, difficulty*			
Qualität (f)	*quality*			
Rassismus (m)	*racism*			
Recht (nt)	*right*			
religiös	*religious*			
respektieren	*(to) respect | respecting*			
schlecht	*bad, badly*			
schmal	*narrow*			
Schokolade (f)	*chocolate*			
Schwester (f)	*sister*			
schwul	*gay*			
sein	*his, its (m, nt)*			
seine	*his, its (f, pl)*			
seltsam	*strange, weird*			
Sexismus (m)	*sexism*			
Situation (f)	*situation*			
Sohn (m)	*son*			
solch	*such*			
Spiel (nt)	*game, match*			
sportlich	*sporty, athletic*			
stattfinden	*(to) take place | taking place*			

Stief- (prefix)	*step-*
streng	*strict, strictly*
süß	*sweet, sweetly*
Tante (f)	*aunt*
tanzen	*(to) dance / dancing*
Teil (m)	*part*
teilen	*(to) share / sharing*
Tochter (f)	*daughter*
Töchter (pl)	*daughters*
Tradition (f)	*tradition*
tragen	*(to) wear, carry / wearing, carrying*
Typ (m)	*type, guy*
überraschen	*(to) surprise / surprising*
übersetzen	*(to) translate / translating*
üblich	*usual*
unabhängig	*independent, independently*
uns	***(to) us (obj)*** */ ourselves (reflex) / each other (recip)*
unser	*our (m, nt)*
unsere	*our (f, pl)*
Unterschied (m)	*difference*
unterschiedlich	*variable, different*
unterstützen	*(to) support / supporting*
Vater (m)	*father*
Veranstaltung (f)	*event*
Verhältnis (nt)	*relationship*
vertrauen	*(to) trust / trusting*
Verwandte (m/f)	*relative, relation*
Vorbild (nt)	*role model*
vorher	*beforehand, earlier*
wenigstens	*at least*
wer	*who?*
Werk (nt)	*work*
Wirklichkeit (f)	*reality*
wohl	*well, happy, probably*
zusammen	*together*
Zwilling (m)	*twin*

Kulturzone Ich liebe Sport

- Using comparative adjectives and adverbs
- H Using superlative adjectives and adverbs

1 Translate these adjectives into English.

1 gut ....
2 hoch ....
3 groß ....
4 nah ....
5 oft ....
6 alt ....
7 jung ....
8 schwach ....
9 stark ....
10 arm ....

2 Complete each sentence using a word from the box.

Bergen	Leichtathletik	
Handball	Sport	Fitnesszentrum

1 Ich laufe gern und mache oft ....
2 Mia läuft auch gern, aber sie spielt auch ab und zu ....
3 Tom geht im Sommer ins Schwimmbad, aber im Winter geht er ins ....

H 4 Aisha geht manchmal in den .... wandern.
H 5 Ich treibe regelmäßig .... und gehe im Sommer häufig schwimmen.

G

The **comparative** is used to **compare** two things: just add ***-er*** to the adjective/adverb and use ***als*** to mean 'than'.

klein – small — *klein**er*** – small**er**
beliebt – popular — *beliebt**er*** – **more** popular

*Die Schweiz ist kleiner **als** Österreich.*
Switzerland is smaller **than** Austria.

Some adjectives are **irregular**:
gut – ***besser***, *viel* – ***mehr***, *gern* – ***lieber***, *hoch* – ***höher***.

One-syllable adjectives often add an umlaut: *groß* – ***größer***, *nah* – ***näher***, *oft* – ***öfter***.

Remember that adjectives need to agree with the noun they are describing:
*Fußball ist ein interessante**rer** Sport als Tennis.*

G

H The **superlative** is used to say something is 'the most ...': add ***-(e)st*** at the end of the adjective and make sure it agrees with the noun.

*Für die Schweizer ist Radfahren der beliebte**ste** Sport.*
For the Swiss, cycling is the **most popular** sport.

Remember that some adjectives are irregular and one-syllable adjectives often add an umlaut.

For superlatives on their own, without a noun after them, use ***am*** before the adjective and add ***-(e)sten*** at the end.

*Dieser Berg ist **am** höch**sten**.*
This mountain is **the highest**.

3 Circle the correct adjective/adverb to complete each sentence.

1 Im Sommer ist es **warm / wärmer** als im Winter.
2 Ich finde Schwimmen **langweiliger / langweilig** als Radfahren.
3 Im deutschen Raum ist Radfahren **beliebt / beliebter** als Wandern.
4 Die Berge sind **näher / nah** an München als an Hamburg.
5 Läufst du auch **lieber / gern** in der Natur als im Fitnesszentrum?

4 Complete these sentences with the correct German comparative form by translating the word(s) in brackets.

1 Ich möchte .... (*more often*) wandern gehen.

2 Die Berge in der Schweiz sind .... (*higher*) als in Deutschland.

3 Ich bin so schwach wie mein Bruder und unsere Schwester ist viel .... (*stronger*) als wir.

4 Ich spiele gut Tennis, aber ich spiele .... (*better*) Handball.

5 Ich spiele viel Tennis, aber ich spiele .... (*more*) Fußball.

H 6 Ich fahre .... (*more frequently*) Rad als meine Stiefschwester.

H 5 Complete each sentence using the correct comparative or superlative form of an adjective/adverb from the box.

arm	hoch	schnell
lang	jung	

1 Meine Schwester ist .... als ich und macht in meiner Familie am meisten Sport.

2 Meine .... Zeit ohne Sport waren zwei Wochen.

3 Mein Halbbruder Sven fährt mindestens dreimal in der Woche Rad und fährt viel .... als ich.

4 Der .... Berg, der zu Deutschland gehört, heißt die Zugspitze.

5 Susanne ist unsere .... Freundin, weil sie nie Geld hat.

F 6 Translate these sentences into German.

1 Swimming in the sea is very popular. ....

2 My brother is older than me. ....

3 Winter is colder than summer. ....

4 I find hiking more boring than cycling. ....

5 I play tennis well, but I play football better. ....

H 7 Translate this paragraph into English.

Meine Familie ist sehr groß, denn wir sind fünf Kinder. Neulich bin ich mit meinem ältesten Bruder und mit meiner jüngsten Schwester in den Bergen Rad gefahren. Ich finde Radfahren spannender als Wandern. Wir sind jeden Tag 70 Kilometer gefahren – das war eine tolle Leistung! Aber es war auch der kälteste Sommer überhaupt!

....

....

....

....

....

....

1 Essen: gesund und gut!

F Giving your opinion in different ways

1 Underline the noun(s) in each sentence and translate them into English.

1. Ich habe immer großen Hunger. ....
2. Ich esse gern Brot mit Ei. ....
3. Ich esse nicht gern Würste. ....
4. Ich möchte bitte ein Stück Käse. ....
5. Ich esse sehr gern Obst. ....

2 Circle the correct form of *mögen* to complete each sentence.

1. Ich habe Durst, aber ich **magst** / **mag** / **mögt** Wasser nicht.
2. Herr Zimmer **mögt** / **magst** / **mag** die Wurst auf dem Tisch nicht.
3. Einige Personen **mögt** / **mögen** / **mag** Eis nicht.
4. Sie sind Kellner hier. **Mag** / **Magst** / **Mögen** Sie das Essen hier im Restaurant?
5. **Mögen** / **Mögt** / **Mag** ihr das Abendessen?

G

mögen (to like) is a modal verb, but it is not always used with an infinitive. It is most commonly used with a noun.

mögen (*to like*)	
ich	mag
du	magst
er/sie/es/man	mag
wir	mögen
ihr	mögt
Sie	mögen
sie	mögen

*Ich **mag** Eis.* I like ice cream.

Remember, to say you like doing something, use ***gern*** after the verb.

*Ich esse **gern** Eis.* I like eating ice cream.

3 Complete these sentences with the correct form of the modal verb *mögen*.

1. Sofia, ... du Kaffee?
2. Nein, aber ich .... Tee.
3. Florian und Brigitte, ... ihr scharfes Essen?
4. Ja, wir .... scharfes Essen.
5. Frau Jansen, ... Sie Kuchen?

4 Translate these sentences into German.

1. I don't like tea.

....

2. I like sausage, but I don't like eating fish.

....

3. I don't like the food here.

....

4. Do you like fruit or do you prefer to eat vegetables?

....

5. I like coffee, but I prefer to drink water.

....

H 1 Complete these German sentences by translating the words in brackets.

1 Die wichtigste .... ist für mich das Frühstück. (*meal*)

2 Ich mag Süßes und esse immer einen ....! (*dessert*)

3 Das Restaurant hat viele leckere .... (*dishes*)

4 Oh nein, die .... ist sauer! (*milk*)

5 Ich möchte bitte mit .... zahlen. (*cash*)

H 2 Separate out the words and write out the sentences.

Add a capital letter to each noun and a comma before *um*.

1 Ichbrauchemesserundgabelumdasschnitzelzuessen.

....

....

2 Ichmöchtebitteeinenlöffelhabenummeinevorspeisezuessen.

....

....

3 Kannichbittedierechnungbekommenumzuzahlen?

....

....

4 Ichessemeinabendessenimmerlangsamumeszugenießen.

....

....

G

H Use the infinitive construction ***um ... zu*** to say '(in order) to'. The infinitive goes to the end of the clause and there is a comma before *um*:

*Ich esse viel, **um** stark **zu** sein.*

I eat a lot **(in order) to** be strong.

With separable verbs, ***zu*** comes in the middle of the word, **after** the separable prefix:

*Ich gehe früh ins Bett, **um** morgen früh auf**zu**stehen.*

I am going to bed early **(in order) to** get up early tomorrow.

H 3 Write full sentences with the words in brackets, using *um ... zu* + infinitive.

1 Ich rufe den Kellner, (*das Essen bestellen*)

....

2 Ich brauche einen sauberen Teller, (*meinen Nachtisch teilen*)

....

3 Der Kellner ist gekommen, („*Guten Appetit*" *sagen*)

....

4 Ich rufe den Kellner, (*ein scharfes Messer bekommen*)

....

H 4 Translate this paragraph into German on a separate sheet.

I never eat breakfast, but the most important meal for me is lunch. I like to eat fish with vegetables. I usually take an hour break. I always take my time in order to eat in peace. After the meal, I have a lot of energy again to learn more.

2 Es geht mir nicht gut

Using modal verbs in the imperfect tense

1 Draw lines to match up the German words with their English translations.

1 der Hals — **a** back
2 der Zahn — **b** heart
3 der Rücken — **c** body
4 der Bauch — **d** neck/throat
H 5 das Herz — **e** stomach
H 6 der Körper — **f** tooth

2 Complete these sentences with the correct German words from the box.

Arm Bein Finger Mund Hand Knochen Fuß Muskeln Haut Augen Nase Schulter

1 Im Gesicht sind die ...., der .... und die .... (*nose, mouth, eyes*)

2 Sie fällt immer vom Fahrrad und bricht sich die .... oder einen .... (*hand, finger*)

3 Ich kann meinen .... und meine .... nicht bewegen. Es tut weh! (*arm, shoulder*)

H 4 Herr Doktor, es geht mir nicht gut. Mein .... und auch mein .... tun weh. (*leg, foot*)

H 5 Ich habe Schmerzen in meinen ...., meiner .... und meinen .... (*muscles, skin, bones*)

G

Modal verbs in the **imperfect tense** have these endings. Note that there is no umlaut on modal verbs in the imperfect tense.

	können (*can, be able to*)	**dürfen** (*may, be allowed to*)	**müssen** (*must, have to*)	**wollen** (*want*)
ich	konn**te**	durf**te**	muss**te**	woll**te**
du	konn**test**	durf**test**	muss**test**	woll**test**
er/sie/es/man	konn**te**	durf**te**	muss**te**	woll**te**

Ich ***konnte*** *(nicht) laufen.* — I could (not) run.
Du ***durftest*** *(nicht) schwimmen.* — You were (not) allowed to swim.
Sie ***musste*** *ins Krankenhaus gehen.* — She had to go to the hospital.
Er ***wollte*** *die Medizin nicht nehmen.* — He did not want to take the medicine.
H *Wir* ***wollten*** *nicht zum Arzt gehen.* — We did not want to go to the doctor.
H *Ihr* ***durftet*** *keinen Sport machen.* — You were not allowed to do sports.
H *Sie* ***konnten*** *nicht laufen.* — You (formal)/They could not run.

3 Circle the correct modal verb to complete each sentence.

1 Ich habe mir vor einem Monat das Knie gebrochen und **musste** / **müssen** / **musstest** eine Woche zu Hause bleiben.

2 Er hatte vor einer Woche Fieber und **konntest** / **konnte** / **können** nicht schlafen.

3 Sie hatte vor zwei Tagen Ohrenschmerzen und **wollen** / **wolltest** / **wollte** nicht in die Schule gehen.

4 Er hatte vor zwei Monaten einen Unfall und **durfte / dürfen / durftest** nicht zur Arbeit gehen.

5 Du hattest vor zwei Tagen Kopfschmerzen und **musste / musstest / müssen** zu Hause bleiben.

Remember that ***vor*** (ago) takes the dative case in German.

***vor** ein**em** Monat*	one month ago
***vor** ein**er** Woche*	one week ago
***vor** ein**em** Jahr*	one year ago
***vor** zwei Wochen*	two weeks ago

4 Complete these sentences with the correct imperfect tense form of the modal verb in brackets. Then translate the verb into English on a separate sheet.

1 Sie war gesund, aber sie .... keinen Fußball spielen. (*dürfen*)

2 Der Unfall ist vor zwei Tagen passiert, aber ich .... nicht zum Arzt gehen. (*wollen*)

3 Du bist vor drei Tagen vom Fahrrad gefallen und .... dich nicht bewegen. (*können*)

4 Er ist gegen Obst allergisch und .... vor zwei Tagen ins Krankenhaus gehen. (*müssen*)

H 5 Ich habe mir vor drei Tagen die Hände verletzt und .... das Blut nicht sehen. (*können*)

H 5 Fill in the missing imperfect tense modal verb in German. Then write down on a separate sheet the English translation of the verb you added.

1 Mein Ohr tut seit einer Woche weh und ich .... letzte Nacht nur wenig schlafen. (*can, be able to*)

2 Ich habe mir vor einer Woche beim Tennisspielen die Schulter verletzt und .... sofort zum Arzt zur Behandlung gehen. (*must, have to*)

seit means '**since**'/'**for**' and takes the dative.

***seit** ein**em** Monat* — for one month

3 Er ist vor fünf Tagen beim Radfahren gefallen und .... zwei Tage nicht in die Schule gehen. (*may, be allowed to*)

4 Sie hatte vor zwei Tagen beim Abendessen Bauchschmerzen, aber sie .... immer mehr essen. (*want*)

5 Du hast dir vor einem Monat beim Fußballspielen den Fuß gebrochen und .... vorsichtig gehen. Aber jetzt sind deine Schmerzen verschwunden! (*must, have to*)

verschwinden (to disappear) is an irregular verb with an inseparable prefix.

F 6 Translate these sentences into English on a separate sheet.

1 Ich muss einen Monat zu Hause bleiben.

2 Vor zwei Tagen hat der Arzt gefragt, „Wie geht's?“

3 Vor einer Woche hatte ich Bauchschmerzen und ich durfte nichts essen.

4 Ich hatte vor sechs Tagen Zahnschmerzen und ich konnte nicht sprechen.

5 Ich wollte heute Morgen Tennis spielen, aber meine Schulter tut weh.

H 7 Translate this paragraph into German on a separate sheet.

Use **beim** + noun to say 'while doing something'. You can change any verb into a neuter noun simply by giving it a capital letter.
*Ich habe mir **beim** Laufen das Bein verletzt.*
I injured my leg **while** running.

Two years ago, I injured my hands while playing handball. I experienced a lot of pain and I had to go to hospital. I wanted to play again immediately, but I wasn't allowed to. I had to stay at home for four weeks. Now the pains have disappeared and I can return to the club.

3 Was möchte ich ändern?

- Revising present, past and future tenses
- **H** Using infinitive constructions with *zu*

1 Translate these verbs into English.

1 sitzen ....

2 reduzieren ....

3 rauchen ....

4 essen ....

5 fernsehen ....

H 6 beschließen ....

H 7 aufgeben ....

2 Draw lines to match up the verbs with their past participles.

1 reduzieren

2 rauchen

3 essen

4 fernsehen

5 beginnen

H 6 sitzen

H 7 beschließen

H 8 aufgeben

a aufgegeben

b ferngesehen

c reduziert

d gegessen

e geraucht

f begonnen

g gesessen

h beschlossen

G

Remember that the **perfect tense** (a past tense) is formed with ***haben*** or ***sein*** + past participle. Some past participles are irregular. The **future tense** is formed with ***werden*** + infinitive.

infinitive	**present tense**	**perfect tense**	**future tense**
sein (*to be*)	ich bin	ich **bin** ... gewesen	ich werde ... sein
schlafen (*to sleep*)	du schläfst	du hast ... geschlafen	du wirst ... schlafen
ändern (*to change, alter*)	er/sie/es/man ändert	er/sie/es/man ... hat geändert	er/sie/es/man wird ... ändern
gehen (*to go, walk*)	wir gehen	wir **sind** ... gegangen	wir werden ... gehen
machen (*to make, do*)	ihr macht	ihr habt ... gemacht	ihr werdet ... machen
bringen (*to bring*)	sie bringen	sie haben ... gebracht	sie werden ... bringen

3 Draw lines to match up the problems with the solutions.

1 Ich habe nicht genug geschlafen.

2 Mein Hund isst zu viel und ist zu dick.

3 Ich habe Rückenschmerzen und ich bin nicht in Form.

4 Ich habe Halsschmerzen und Augenschmerzen – es tut weh!

5 Ich trinke nicht genug und kann mich nicht konzentrieren.

a Ich werde mehr Wasser trinken, das hilft.

b Ich werde mich mehr bewegen und wieder in Form sein.

c Er wird sich mehr bewegen.

d Eine bessere Zeit hat begonnen und ich werde früher ins Bett gehen.

e Ich werde mein Handy weniger benutzen.

4 Rewrite these sentences in the perfect tense.

1 Ich kaufe zu viel Fastfood. ....

2 Ich benutze mein Handy weniger dazu. ....

3 Ich esse gesünder. ....

4 Ich rauche weniger. ....

H 5 Ich werde weniger Zeit vor dem Bildschirm verbringen.

....

H **5 Complete these sentences by translating the word(s) in brackets into German.**

Think about the form of the word you need in German.

1 Ich habe begonnen, das Problem zu .... (*solve*)

2 Ich habe beschlossen, gesünder zu .... (*live*)

3 Ich werde es schaffen, mehr Obst und Gemüse dazu zu .... (*eat*)

4 Ich habe eine Veränderung gebraucht und die Zeit vor dem Bildschirm .... (*reduce*)

5 Ich habe Fastfood und das Rauchen .... (*give up*)

G

H Some verbs require the addition of ***zu*** before an infinitive.
*Ich beginne, mehr Sport **zu** machen.*
I am beginning to do more sport.
*Ich beschließe/entscheide/habe vor/plane/versuche/verspreche, ... **zu** ...*
I decide/intend/plan/try/promise to ...
Modal verbs do not follow this pattern and **do not** need ***zu*** before an infinitive:
*Ich **muss** mehr Sport machen.*

F **6 Translate these sentences into German.**

1 I don't drink enough water. ....

2 Now I eat more healthily. ....

3 In the future I will watch less TV. ....

4 Two weeks ago I was not active. ....

5 I have pains because I spend too much time on my mobile phone.

....

H **7 Translate this paragraph into English.**

Ich kann mich nicht konzentrieren, weil ich nicht genug schlafe und zu müde bin. Aber ich habe beschlossen, das zu ändern! Ich verspreche, früher ins Bett zu gehen. Ich habe es schon geschafft, die Zeit vor dem Bildschirm zu reduzieren! In der Zukunft werde ich mich auch mehr bewegen und gesünder essen.

....

....

....

....

....

4 Gute Tage, schlechte Tage

F Using *wenn* + present tense

1 Underline the verbs in each sentence. Write down their infinitive forms and translate them into English.

1. Ich weine, weil ich traurig bin. ......
2. Ich mache Sport, weil ich wenig Energie habe. ......
3. Ich bleibe zu Hause, weil das Wetter schlecht ist. ......
4. Ich höre klassische Musik, weil ich gestresst bin. ......
5. Ich spreche mit meinen Eltern, weil ich Schwierigkeiten in der Schule habe.

   ......

2 Separate out the words and write out the sentences. Insert the comma in the correct place.

1. WennichtraurigbinsprecheichmitmeinerSchwester.

   ......
2. WenndasWetterschlechtistliestsieeinBuch.

   ......
3. WennmeinFreundkrankistnimmterMedizin.

   ......
4. WennichProblemehaberufeichmeineFreundean.

   ......
5. WennichkeineEnergiehabemacheichzweiStundenSport.

   ......
6. Wenn icheineschwierigeWochehabegeheichspazieren.

   ......

> **G**
> **H** The conjunction **wenn** can mean 'when', 'whenever' or 'if', and is used to express what you do in certain situations. Note the **verb–comma–verb** structure:
> ***Wenn*** *ich nicht glücklich* ***bin, chatte*** *ich mit Freunden.*
> **When** I **am** not happy, I **chat** with friends.

3 Rewrite each sentence on a separate sheet, putting the words into the correct order.

1. Bergen / das / ich / Wetter / ist, / den / wandern. / Wenn / schön / in / gehe
2. meiner / gibt, / spreche / mit / Wenn es / Lehrerin. / Konflikte / ich
3. habe, / Geld / ins / Wenn / gehe / genug / ich / Kino. / ich
4. schlafe, / glücklich. / bin / gut / ich / ich / Wenn
5. Wenn / geht / meine / ich / treffe, / es / besser. / Freunde / mir

> ★
> - Each sentence starts with *Wenn.*
> - Look for the words with a comma or full stop to help you organise the sentences. Remember the verb–comma–verb structure.

4 Translate these sentences into German on a separate sheet.

1. I have little energy.
2. Sometimes I have problems with my parents.
3. Whenever I'm too thin, I eat more.
4. When you fall, you call your grandmother.
5. If you break your arm, you go to the doctor.

> ★
> Remember that with present tense separable verbs, the prefix comes at the end of the clause.

4 Gute Tage, schlechte Tage

- **H** Using *wenn* + imperfect subjunctive and conditional
- **H** Using set phrases with *zu*

Module 4
Student Book pp. 88–89

H 1 Complete each sentence using a word from the box.

positive
stolz
erkennen
enthalten
sinnvoll
körperliche

1 Bewegung ist gut für die .... Gesundheit.

2 Eine .... Einstellung ist wichtig für die geistige Gesundheit.

3 Es ist .... und hilft sehr, über Probleme zu sprechen.

4 Du kannst .... auf dich sein, denn du hast die Hoffnung nicht aufgegeben.

5 Wir müssen ...., dass eine negative Einstellung nicht gut für uns ist.

6 Jede Mahlzeit muss Gemüse ...., weil das gesund ist.

H 2 Complete each sentence using a verb from the box.

wäre wäre würde
habe hätte hätte

1 Wenn ich aktiver wäre, ... ich mich besser fühlen und weniger Schmerzen kriegen.

2 Wenn ich nicht so oft traurig ...., würde ich mich nicht verstecken, sondern mehr lachen.

3 Wenn ich eine Schwester ...., würde ich mit ihr über meine Probleme sprechen.

4 Wenn ich positiver wäre, ... ich mehr Hoffnung und mir würde alles gelingen.

5 Wenn ich ein Haustier hätte, würde mir das Freude bringen und ich .... glücklich.

6 Wenn ich Freizeit ...., treibe ich Sport.

G

H The conjunction ***wenn*** is often used together with the imperfect subjunctive (***hätte***, ***wäre***) and **conditional** (***würde***) to express what you **would** do **if** you **had …** or **if** you **were …**

*Wenn ich mehr Zeit **hätte, würde** ich mehr lesen.*
If I **had** more time, I **would** read more.
*Wenn ich weniger traurig **wäre, würde** ich mehr lachen.*
If I **were** less sad, I **would** laugh more.
Note the **verb–comma–verb** structure and the infinitive at the end of the sentence.

wenn also means '**when**' and can be used with the present tense:
***Wenn** das Wetter gut ist, gehe ich spazieren.*
When the weather is good, I go for a walk.

H 3 Draw lines to match up the sentence halves.

1 Wenn ich Probleme hätte,
2 Wenn ich müde wäre,
3 Wenn ich allein und traurig wäre,
4 Wenn ich eine positive Einstellung hätte,

a würde ich alte Fotos von meiner Familie betrachten.
b wäre ich glücklicher und würde mehr lachen.
c würde ich mehr schlafen.
d würde ich mit jemandem darüber sprechen.

H ***zu*** + infinitive is used with a number of phrases containing an adjective and the verb ***sein***:
Es ist wichtig, positiv zu sein.
It is important to be positive.
Es ist sinnvoll, (useful) / *nötig*, (necessary) / *schwierig*, (difficult) …

H 4 Translate this paragraph into German on a separate sheet.

It is important for physical and mental health to have a positive attitude. If there are problems, it's useful to talk about them. If I didn't have a best friend, I would be sad. It is necessary to be active. If I had time, I would go to the fitness centre regularly.

5 Das finde ich wichtig!

Understanding questions in different tenses

1 Unjumble the letters to rewrite the words correctly. Add the definite article (*der, die* or *das*). Then write the English translations next to the German words.

1 othRslllu ....

2 scanhMnaft ....

3 aKrrriee ....

4 ndesuehGit ....

H 5 Snin ....

H 6 rWte ....

2 Draw lines to match up the questions with the answers.

1 Machst du Sport?

2 Isst du gesund?

3 Ist eine Karriere wichtig für dich?

H 4 Bist du erfolgreich?

H 5 Was ist wichtig für dich?

a Ja, ich esse viel Obst und Gemüse.

b Ja, aber meine Gesundheit ist mir wichtiger

c Ja, ich spiele in einer Mannschaft Handball.

H **d** Persönliche Werte und eine gute Karriere.

H **e** Ja, aber ich möchte erwähnen, dass ich auch viel Druck habe.

G

Remember:
Use the **present tense** to talk about what you **do** or **are doing now**:
***Isst** du Obst?* **Do** you **eat** fruit? / **Are** you **eating** fruit?

Use the **perfect** and **imperfect tenses** to talk about something that happened in the **past**:
***Hast** du Obst **gegessen**?* Did you **eat** fruit?
***Bist** du in den Park **gegangen**?* Did you go to the park?
***Hattest** du Obst?* **Did** you **have** fruit?
***Warst** du im Park?* Were you in the park?

Use the **future tense** to talk about something that will happen in the **future**:
***Wirst** du Obst **essen**?* **Will** you **eat** fruit?

3 Underline the verb(s) in each question. Then write which tense each question is in: past (P), present (Pr) or future (F).

1 Was macht dir Freude? ☐

2 Wirst du auf Berge steigen? ☐

3 Bist du stolz auf dich? ☐

4 Wann hast du zum letzten Mal ein Buch gelesen? ☐

5 Lebst du normalerweise gesund? ☐

6 Was hast du gemacht, wenn du traurig warst? ☐

7 Was wirst du nach der Schule machen? ☐

4 Complete these German questions and their English translations.

1 .... nach der Schule gemacht?

What did you ....?

2 Ist Tieren helfen .... ?

.... *important to you?*

3 ...., wenn du gestresst bist?

What do you do ....?

H **4** .... einen Wettbewerb haben?

Will you ....?

H **5** .... mit dem Erfolg gestiegen?

Has the pressure ....?

H **5 Draw lines to match up the questions with the answers.**

1 Ist eine gute Ausbildung erhalten wichtig für dich?

2 Wirst du nach der Schule an die Universität gehen?

3 Warum wirst du dir einen Job suchen?

4 Was hast du mit dem Geld von Opa gemacht?

5 Wirst du Sportschuhe mitnehmen?

6 Was hat deine Familie dazu gesagt?

a Ja, falls ich wandern gehe.

b Meine Mutter begann, zu weinen. Meine Schwester dagegen hat die Idee gut gefunden und mich gebeten, viele Fotos zu machen.

c Nein, ich werde mir einen Job suchen.

d Ich beobachte gern Tiere und habe mir eine Ausrüstung gekauft.

e Ja, allerdings finde ich Reisen wichtiger.

f Ich werde reisen und ich brauche Geld dafür.

F **6 Translate these sentences into English.**

1 Wie wichtig ist dir die Schule? ....

2 Was hast du letzte Woche für deine Familie gemacht? ....

3 Was ist dir wichtiger, eine gute Arbeit finden oder Abenteuer haben? ....

....

4 Wirst du in der Zukunft mehr Sport machen? ....

5 Bist du gestern laufen gegangen? ....

H **7 Translate this paragraph into German on a separate sheet.**

What is important to me? Success and a career were the most important things for me in the past. But now I am trying to find a purpose and to have a positive attitude. I would also like to comment that it is meaningful to have good friends. I hope to have less pressure.

Glossary

bold = this word will appear in Higher exams only

		😐	🙂	😎
Abendessen (nt)	*dinner, supper, evening meal*			
allerdings	*though, indeed*			
allergisch	*allergic*			
am höchsten	*(the) highest (post-noun)*			
am meisten	*(the) most (post-noun)*			
Arm (m)	*arm*			
aufgeben	*(to) give up / giving up*			
Auge (nt)	*eye*			
Ausrüstung (f)	*equipment, gear*			
Ball (m)	*ball*			
Bargeld (nt)	*cash*			
Bauch (m)	*stomach, belly*			
begann	*(I/she, he, it) began, started*			
(aux) ... begonnen	*began, started / (have, has) begun, started*			
Behandlung (f)	*treatment*			
Bein (nt)	*leg*			
bemerken	*(to) notice, remark, comment / noticing, remarking, commenting*			
beobachten	*(to) observe, watch / observing, watching*			
beschließen	*(to) decide / deciding*			
bestellen	*(to) order / ordering*			
betrachten	*(to) look at, consider / looking at, considering*			
(sich) bewegen	*(to) move, exercise / moving, exercising*			
Bewegung (f)	*exercise, movement*			
Bildschirm (m)	*screen, monitor*			
Blut (nt)	*blood*			
brechen	*(to) break / breaking*			
brichst	*(you (sing informal)) break / are breaking*			
bricht	*(she, he, it, one) breaks / is breaking*			
Brot (nt)	*bread, loaf*			
dafür	***for it, for that***			
dagegen	*against it, on the other hand*			
dazu	***to that, for that,*** *in addition,* ***furthermore***			
der/die/das älteste	*(the) oldest*			
der/die/das ärmste	*(the) poorest*			
der/die/das jüngste	*(the) youngest*			
der/die/das kälteste	*(the) coldest*			
der/die/das längste	*(the) longest*			
der/die/das beste	*the best (pre-noun)*			
der/die/das höchste	*the highest (pre-noun)*			
der/die/das nächste	*the next, nearest (pre-noun)*			
dick	*thick, fat*			
Doktor (m)	*doctor*			
Druck (m)	*pressure*			
dünn	*thin, thinly*			
durfte	*(I/she, he, it, one) was allowed to*			
durftest	*(you (sing informal)) were allowed to*			

Durst (m)	*thirst*
Ei (nt)	*egg*
Einstellung (f)	*attitude*
Eis (nt)	*ice, ice cream*
Energie (f)	*energy, power*
enthalten	*(to) contain | containing*
erhalten	*(to) receive | receiving*
erkennen	*(to) recognise | recognising*
erwähnen	*(to) mention | mentioning*
Es geht mir ...	*I am ..., I feel ...*
es tut weh	*it hurts*
Essen (nt)	*food, meal, eating*
fährt	*(she, he, it) goes (by transport), drives, travels*
fallen	*(to) fall | falling*
falls	*in case, if*
fällst	*(you (sing informal)) fall | are falling*
fällt	*(she, he, it, one) falls | is falling*
Fastfood (nt)	*fast food*
Fieber (nt)	*fever, high temperature*
Finger (m)	*finger*
Fitnesszentrum (nt)	*gym*
Form (f); in Form	*form, shape; in shape, fit*
Freude (f)	*joy*
früher	*previously, in former times, in the past*
(sich) fühlen	*(to) feel | feeling*
Fuß (m); zu Fuß	*foot; on foot, walking*
Gabel (f)	*fork*
(aux) ... gebeten	*requested, asked (for) / (have, has) requested, asked (for)*
(aux) ... gebracht	*brought / (have, has) brought*
gehören	*(to) belong (to) | belonging (to)*
geistig	*mental, psychological*
gelingen	*(to) succeed | succeeding*
Gemüse (nt)	*vegetable, vegetables*
Gericht (nt)	*dish, course*
Gesicht (nt)	*face*
gesund	*healthy, healthily*
gesünder	*healthier*
Gesundheit (f)	*health*
größer	*bigger*
Guten Appetit!	*Enjoy your meal!*
Hals (m)	*neck, throat*
Hand (f)	*hand*
Handball (m)	*handball*
Hände (pl)	*hands*
hast	*(you (sing informal)) have | are having*
hätte	*(I/she, she, he, it) had / would have*
Haut (f)	*skin*
heißen	*(to) be called, mean | being called, meaning*
helfen	*(to) help | helping*
Herr (m)	*Mr, gentleman*
Herz (nt)	*heart*
hilft	*(she, he, it, one) helps | is helping*
Hoffnung (f)	*hope*
höher	*higher, taller*
Hunger (m)	*hunger*
ist	*(she, he, it, one) is | is being*
Kaffee (m)	*coffee*
Karriere (f)	*career*
Käse (m)	*cheese*

Kellner (m)	*waiter*			
Knie (nt)	*knee*			
Knochen (m)	*bone*			
Konflikt (m)	*conflict*			
konnte	*(I/she, he, it, one) was able to, could*			
konntest	*(you (sing informal)) were able to, could*			
(sich) konzentrieren (auf)	*(to) concentrate (on) / concentrating (on)*			
Kopf (m)	*head*			
Körper (m)	*body*			
körperlich	*physical, physically*			
Krankenhaus (nt)	*hospital*			
kriegen	*(to) get, receive / getting, receiving*			
läufst	*(you (sing informal)) run / are running*			
läuft	*(she, he, it, one) runs / is running*			
Leichtathletik (f)	*athletics, track and field*			
Leistung (f)	*achievement, performance*			
liest	*(you (sing informal)) read / are reading / (she, he, it, one) reads / is reading*			
Löffel (m)	*spoon*			
lösen	*(to) solve / solving*			
Mahlzeit (f)	*meal*			
Mannschaft (f)	*team*			
mehr	*more*			
Messer (nt)	*knife*			
Milch (f)	*milk*			
mindestens	*at least*			
Monat (m)	*month*			
müde	*tired*			
Mund (m)	*mouth*			
Muskel (m)	*muscle*			
musste	*(I/she, he, it, one) had to*			
musstest	*(you (sing informal)) had to*			
Nachtisch (m)	*dessert*			
näher	*nearer*			
Nase (f)	*nose*			
negativ	*negative*			
nehmen	*(to) take / taking*			
nimmt	*(she, he, it, one) takes / is taking*			
Obst (nt)	*fruit*			
Ohr (nt)	*ear*			
Ohren (pl)	*ears*			
passieren	*(to) happen / happening*			
Person (f)	*person*			
persönlich	*personal, personally*			
positiv	*positive, positively*			
rauchen	*(to) smoke / smoking*			
Raum (m)	*room, space*			
reduzieren	*(to) reduce / reducing*			
regelmäßig	*regular, regularly*			
Rollstuhl (m)	*wheelchair*			
Rücken (m)	*back*			
sauer	*sour*			
schaffen	*(to) manage / managing*			
scharf	*sharp, sharply, spicy, spicily*			
Schmerz (m)	*pain*			
Schmerzen (pl)	*pains*			
Schnitzel (nt)	*schnitzel, escalope*			
Schulter (f)	*shoulder*			
schwach	*weak, weakly*			
Schweizer	*Swiss, Swiss man*			

		😕	🙂	😎
Schwierigkeit (f)	*difficulty*			
schwimmen	*(to) swim | swimming*			
seit	*since, for*			
Sinn (m)	*sense, meaning*			
sinnvoll	*meaningful, meaningfully*			
sitzen	*(to) sit | sitting*			
so … wie	*as … as*			
sofort	*immediately, at once*			
sondern	*(but) rather*			
stark	*strong, strongly*			
steigen	*(to) climb, rise, increase | climbing, rising, increasing*			
stolz (auf)	*proud (of), proudly*			
Stück (nt)	*piece, play*			
Stunde (f)	*lesson, hour, class*			
Tee (m)	*tea*			
Teller (m)	*plate*			
Tennis (nt)	*tennis*			
Tisch (m)	*table*			
treiben	*(to) drive, pursue (do sport) | driving, pursuing (doing sport)*			
tun	*(to) do, put | doing, putting*			
um … zu (+ infinitive)	*in order to (+ verb)*			
Unfall (m)	*accident*			
Veränderung (f)	*change*			
(sich) verletzen	*(to) injure (oneself), hurt | injuring (oneself), hurting*			
verschwinden	*(to) disappear | disappearing*			
versprechen	*(to) promise | promising*			
(sich) verstecken	*(to) hide | hiding*			
vorsichtig	*careful, carefully*			
Vorspeise (f)	*starter*			
wäre	*(I/she, he, it) were | would be*			
wärmer	*warmer*			
Wasser (nt)	*water*			
weinen	*(to) cry, weep | crying, weeping*			
wenig	*little*			
wenn	*if, whenever, when*			
Wert (m)	*value, worth*			
Wettbewerb (m)	*competition*			
Wie geht's?	*How are you?*			
wollte	*(I/she, he, it, one) wanted (to)*			
Wurst (f)	*sausage*			
Würste (pl)	*sausages*			
Zahl (f)	*figure, number*			
zahlen	*(to) pay | paying*			
Zahn (m)	*tooth*			

Kulturzone Wo spricht man Deutsch?

Revising the comparative • H Revising the superlative

1 Draw lines to match up the German with the English nouns.

1 die Größe	**a** height
2 die Höhe	**b** country
3 die Lage	**c** language
4 das Land	**d** size
5 die Öffentlichkeit	**e** public
6 die Sprache	**f** location

2 Complete each German sentence using an adjective from the box.

hoch tot
kalt lang
zentral groß
niedrig freundlich

1 Der Berg ist sehr .... *The mountain is very high.*

2 Das Wetter ist .... *The weather is cold.*

3 Der Fluss ist sehr .... *The river is very long.*

4 Die Stadt ist sehr ....
The town is very central.

5 Das Land ist sehr ....
The country is very big.

H **6** Die Bäume sind ....
The trees are dead.

H **7** Die Bevölkerung ist ....
The population is low.

H **8** Die Einwohner sind ....
The inhabitants are friendly.

G

Use the **comparative** to compare things, people and places.

To form the comparative, add *-er* to the adjective and use *als* to say 'than'.

Some adjectives also add an umlaut to the vowel in the comparative.

klein → *klein**er***

*Der Junge ist klein**er** als der Mann.*

The boy is smaller than the man.

lang → *l**ä**ng**er***

*Die Donau ist l**ä**ng**er** als der Rhein.*

The Danube is longer than the Rhine.

3 Complete these sentences with the correct comparative form of the verb in brackets. Then translate the sentences into English.

1 Der Fluss ist .... als der Rhein. (*lang*)

....

2 Das Wetter ist .... als in Deutschland. (*kalt*)

....

3 Die Stadt ist .... als das Dorf. (*groß*)

....

4 Der Mann ist .... als der Junge. (*alt*)

....

5 Das Mädchen ist .... als die Frau. (*klein*)

....

6 Die Berge sind .... als in Österreich. (*hoch*)

....

4 Write out these numbers in words in German.

1 550 ....

....

2 398 ....

....

3 2 025 ....

....

4 4 635 ....

....

5 1 997

....

6 41 285

....

You need to know how to form large numbers in German.
500 – fünfhundert
1000 – (ein)tausend
5000 – fünftausend
2015 – zweitausendfünfzehn
33 679 – dreiunddreißigtausend-sechshundertneunundsiebzig
German uses small spaces or a full stop to separate thousands, and a comma as a decimal point – the opposite of the format used in English!

H 5 Complete these sentences with the correct superlative form of the adjective in brackets. Then translate the sentences into English on a separate piece of paper.

1 Das ist das .... Schloss. (*groß*)

2 Bern ist die .... Hauptstadt. (*alt*)

3 Die Donau ist der .... Fluss. (*lang*)

4 Das Matterhorn ist der .... Berg. (*hoch*)

5 Luxemburg hat die .... Bevölkerung. (*niedrig*)

6 Liechtenstein ist das .... Land. (*klein*)

G

H Use the **superlative** to say 'the most' or 'the least'.
To form the superlative, add -*(e)ste* to the adjective.
Some adjectives also add umlauts to the vowel.
The adjective needs to agree with the noun it's describing.
*der h**ö**ch**ste** Punkt* the highest point
*das **ä**lt**este** Schloss* the oldest castle

F 6 Translate these sentences into German.

1 I live in Austria. ....

2 Where do you come from? ....

3 The national holiday is in October. ....

4 Vienna is bigger than Cologne. ....

5 In the winter it is colder than in Germany. ....

H 7 Translate this paragraph into English.

Meine Heimat ist die Schweiz. Die meisten Leute wohnen in Zürich, obwohl die Hauptstadt Bern ist und Bern kleiner als Zürich ist. Der längste Fluss ist 292 km lang und er geht durch die Stadtmitte. Der Nationaltag ist am ersten August und wir haben oft gefeiert. Der höchste Berg ist 4 478 m hoch.

....

....

....

....

1 Wo wohnst du?

- Using prepositions followed by the dative
- Using a variety of adjectives with intensifiers and qualifiers

1 Choose the correct English translation by selecting a word/phrase from the box. There are more words/phrases than you need.

1 der Bahnhof ....
2 die Bank ....
3 das Feld ....
4 der Flughafen ....
5 die Post ....
6 das Stadion ....
7 die Schule ....
8 die Universität ....

post office
field
university
airport
castle
station
swimming pool
bank
school
stadium

2 Circle the correct word to complete each translation.

1 Das Dorf ist sehr sauber. *The village is very **new** / **clean**.*
2 Die Stadt ist nicht schmutzig. *The town isn't **dirty** / **quiet**.*
3 Die Gegend ist ziemlich multikulturell. *The **area** / **population** is quite multicultural.*
4 Die Stadtmitte ist echt alt. *The town centre is really **old** / **loud**.*
H 5 Die Umgebung ist ganz historisch. *The **buildings** / **surroundings** are quite historical.*
H 6 Der Bereich ist echt sicher. *The area is really **dirty** / **safe**.*

3 Complete these sentences by translating the words in brackets into German.

1 Die Nachbarn sind .... (*quite friendly*)
2 Das Dorf ist .... (*really quiet*)
3 Die Stadt ist .... (*quite dirty*)
4 Das einzige Geschäft ist .... (*really new*)
H 5 Die öffentlichen Gebäude sind .... (*quite old*)
H 6 Der Verkehr ist ein .... (*very big problem*)

G
Use **intensifiers** or **qualifiers** to make an adjective weaker or stronger.
*Das ist **ziemlich** laut.* That is **quite** loud.
*Das ist **ganz** modern.* That is **quite** modern.
*Das ist **echt** ruhig.* That is **really** quiet.

4 Read the grammar box on the next page. Complete these German sentences with the correct article.

1 Ich komme aus .... Dorf (*nt*) im Westen. *I come from a village in the west.*
2 Die Straße nach .... Schule (*f*) ist sehr breit. *The street after the school is very wide.*
3 Die Fahrt von .... Brücke (*f*) her ist sehr kurz. *The trip here from the bridge is very short.*
4 Die Universität befindet sich bei .... Fluss (*m*). *The university is situated by a river.*
5 Ich gehe mit .... Familie (*f*). *I go with the family.*
H 6 Das Museum ist gegenüber .... Krankenhaus (*nt*). *The museum is opposite the hospital.*

G

Some **prepositions** are **always** followed by the **dative**:

ab from
aus out of, from
bei at, near, by
mit with
nach after, to, according to
von from, by, of, about
zu to
H *außer* except
H *gegenüber* opposite
H *seit* since

*Ich wohne **mit meiner** Großmutter.* I live with my grandmother.
*Ich komme **aus der** Stadt.* I come from the town.
*Ich lebe **bei einem** Fluss.* I live by a river.
*Die Schule befindet sich **gegenüber dem** Schloss.* The school is situated opposite the castle.

	masculine	feminine	neuter	plural
definite article: 'the'	dem	der	dem	den
indefinite article: 'a', 'an'	einem	einer	einem	–
negatives	keinem	keiner	keinem	keinen
possessive adjectives	meinem	meiner	meinem	meinen

When *bei* and *von* are followed by *dem*, they change: *bei* + *dem* = *beim*; *von* + *dem* = *vom*.

When *zu* is followed by *der* or *dem*, it changes: *zu* + *der* = *zur*; *zu* + *dem* = *zum*.

5 Circle the correct article to complete each sentence. Then translate the sentences into English on a separate sheet.

1 Es gibt **einen** / **ein** / **eine** Feld (*nt*).
2 Es gibt **keinen** / **kein** / **keine** Kino (*nt*).
3 Es gibt **einen** / **ein** / **eine** Schule (*f*).
4 Es gibt **keinen** / **kein** / **keine** Bahnhof (*m*).
5 Es gab **einen** / **ein** / **eine** Theater (*nt*).
6 Es gab **keinen** / **kein** / **keine** Universität (*f*).

G

Es gibt is always followed by the **accusative**.
*Es gibt **einen** Flughafen.* There is an airport.
*Es gibt **ein** Geschäft.* There is a shop.
*Es gibt **keine** Bank.* There is no bank.

F 6 Translate these sentences into English.

1 Ich wohne in einem sehr kleinen Dorf. ....
2 Wohnst du mit deiner Familie? ....
3 Es gibt keinen Bahnhof. ....
4 Im Süden gibt es eine Post. ....
5 Es gibt nichts für junge Leute. ....

H 7 Translate this paragraph into German.

My town is situated in the east of Germany. I live on the edge of a small town. There is no castle but there is a cinema opposite the school. There was a theatre but it is now closed. The area is very multicultural and quite clean. I really like living here.

....
....
....
....
....

2 Wie fährst du?

Using prepositions with the accusative • Using correct word order

1 Draw lines to match up the sentence halves.

1 Die Reise dauert	**a** als das Fahrrad.
2 Ich komme mit	**b** öffentlichen Bussen.
3 Ich reise	**c** Flugzeug.
4 Die Schule ist	**d** dem Auto nach Hause.
5 Der Zug ist schneller	**e** mit einem privaten Bus.
6 Ich fahre mit den	**f** zwei Stunden.
H 7 Ich fliege mit dem	**g** ganz nah.

★ Use the glossary to look up any words that are unfamiliar, and try to learn them.

G

Some **prepositions** are **always** followed by the **accusative**.

bis until, up to
durch through
für for
ohne without
H *um* around
H *gegen* against
H *entlang* along (goes after the noun)

Die Straße geht ***durch die*** *Stadt.*
The road goes through the town.

Ich kaufe ein Geschenk ***für meinen*** *Vater.* I buy a present for my dad.

Masculine nouns change their articles in the accusative.

masculine		
	the	***a/an***
nominative	der	ein
accusative	de**n**	ein**en**

2 Complete these German sentences with the correct preposition and article.

1 He leads the horses through the village.	*Er führt die Pferde* .... *Dorf (nt).*
2 That's a present for my brother.	*Das ist ein Geschenk* .... *Bruder (m).*
3 She drives without her dad.	*Sie fährt* .... *Vater (m).*
4 Why are you driving around the corner?	*Warum fährst du* .... *Ecke (f)?*
H 5 I put the picture against the wall.	*Ich stelle das Bild* .... *Wand (f).*
H 6 We drive along the street.	*Wir fahren* .... *Straße (f)* ....

G

Here are some key word order rules to remember:

- First comes **time**, then **manner**, then **place**.
- The verb is always the second idea of the sentence.
- A modal verb sends the second verb (the infinitive) to the end of the clause.
- Some conjunctions such as **weil** (because) and ***obwohl*** (although) send the verb to the end of the clause:

Ich will mit dem Wagen fahren, ***weil*** *das schnell* ***ist****.* I want to go by car because that is fast.

Ich fahre gern mit dem Zug, ***obwohl*** *das teuer* ***ist****.* I like going by train although it is expensive.

3 Rewrite each sentence, putting the words into the correct order.

1 Deutschland Ich will machen eine Reise nach ....

....

2 Die dauern Fahrt eine Stunde kann ....

....

3 Sie nach Hause immer fährt mit dem Auto ....

....

4 Nächstes mit dem Zug in die Ferien Wochenende fahren wir ....

....

5 Ich Rad, fahre gern mit weil langsam ist das dem ....

....

6 reisen oft Flugzeug, mit dem das bequem weil ist Wir ....

....

H 4 Join the sentences using the conjunction in brackets. Remember to change the word order in the subordinate clause.

1 Sie fährt nicht gern mit dem Bus. Das kann billig sein. (*obwohl*)

....

2 Sie reisen gar nicht gern mit dem Boot. Das kann praktisch sein. (*obwohl*)

....

3 Ihr fahrt oft mit dem Zug. Das muss sehr schnell sein. (*weil*)

....

4 Ich fahre lieber mit einem Fahrzeug. Die Schule ist sehr weit entfernt. (*weil*)

....

5 Ich muss den Bus erreichen. Ich will nicht spät ankommen. (*weil*)

....

6 Ich fahre jeden Tag mit der Straßenbahn. Das ist sehr teuer. (*obwohl*)

....

In exercises 3 and 4, try to work out the English translation of the sentences. Look up any words you don't know and try to learn them.

F 5 Translate these sentences into German.

1 I like travelling by bike. ....

2 How do you like to travel? ....

3 We like going by bus because it's cheap. ....

4 The journey can last an hour. ....

5 He's driving around the corner. ....

H 6 Translate this paragraph into English.

Ich fahre oft mit dem Rad, weil ich das mag. Wenn ich in die Ferien fahre, reise ich lieber mit dem Schiff, obwohl das langsam ist. Man kann viele Sachen sehen. Wir fahren mit der Straßenbahn in die Stadt, weil das am schnellsten ist. Die öffentlichen Busse sind sehr schmutzig.

....

....

....

....

....

3 Ich komme zu Besuch

Understanding register

1 Write the words in the correct columns. Some words might fit more than one category.

die Brücke	die Ecke	die Fahrkarte	die Franken	die Hose	die Kasse
H das Kilogramm	H der Preis	der Pullover	die Rückfahrkarte	die Tasche	links
der Straßenplan	direkt	frisch	rechts	geradeaus	

Buying tickets at the train station	Asking for directions	Buying food at the market	Buying clothes at the clothes shop

2 Complete each German question using a question word from the box.

Was Wann
Warum Welch-
Wer Wie
Wie viel Wo
Woher Wohin

1 .... wohnst du? *Where do you live?*

2 .... kommst du? *Where do you come from?*

3 .... ist das? *Who is that?*

4 Um .... Uhr kommt der Zug an? *At what time does the train arrive?*

5 .... fährst du? *How are you going?*

6 .... kostet das? *What does it cost?*

7 .... fährst du mit dem Bus? *Why do you go by bus?*

H 8 Ab .... Bahnhof fährt der Zug? *From which station does the train leave?*

G

It is important to know when to use each of the words for 'you' in German.

- Use ***du*** when talking to one person we know well or who is younger than us.
- Use ***ihr*** when talking to a group of people we know well or who are younger than us.
- Use ***Sie*** when being formal, talking to people we don't know or who are older than us.

Which word for 'you' would you use for talking to:

- a friend?
- a group of friends?
- a shopkeeper you don't know?

G

There are different ways of asking questions in German:

- using a question word such as those in exercise 2
- swapping over the subject and the verb.

Wie *kommt man zum Schwimmbad?*
How do I get to the swimming pool?
Wo *liegt das Schwimmbad?*
Where is the swimming pool situated?
Ist das Schwimmbad *in der Nähe?*
Is the swimming pool nearby?

3 Underline the word for 'you' in each sentence or question. Then translate the sentences into English.

1 Haben Sie frische Ware? ....

2 Weißt du das? ....

3 Kommt ihr mit? ....

4 Du musst in diese Richtung gehen. ....

5 Ihr spielt Tennis einmal pro Tag. ....

H 6 Sie sollen weitergehen. ....

H 7 Entschuldigung! Haben Sie Kleingeld? ....

4 Draw lines to match up the questions with the answers.

1 Entschuldigung, wie komme ich zur Schule?
2 Sind die Kosten hoch?
3 Ist das eine sehr lange Strecke?
4 Um wie viel Uhr kommst du zurück?
5 Ist das Theater in der Nähe?
H 6 Wann fährt die U-Bahn ab?

a Ja, das ist ziemlich lang.
b Gehen Sie geradeaus und die Schule ist auf der linken Seite.
c Sie fährt um neun Uhr ab.
d Ja, das kostet viel Geld.
e Nein, das liegt ganz weit weg.
f Ich komme um halb elf zurück.

H 5 Write questions in German for these answers.

1 Die Brücke ist ganz fern. ....
2 Für Erwachsene kostet eine Fahrkarte zwanzig Franken. ....
3 Generell fahre ich mit dem Auto. ....
4 Die Treppe ist ganz eng. ....
5 Die Bank ist um neun Uhr offen. ....
6 Das ist ein Zeichen, dass das Wetter heiß ist. ....

F 6 Translate these sentences into English.

1 Ich möchte mit dem Zug fahren. ....
2 Ist der Zug direkt? ....
3 Ich komme mit, weil das Spaß macht. ....
4 Gehen Sie geradeaus und das Kino befindet sich auf der rechten Seite. ....
....
5 Die Ladung kostet zehn Franken. ....

H 7 Translate this paragraph into German.

I like to travel by tram, but a return ticket is quite expensive. How do you most like to travel? From the station my house is not far, but the streets are narrow. Generally, I do my shopping at the supermarket and I buy two kilogrammes of fruit per day.

In German, you don't need a word for 'of' with weights of items. Here, you need to translate 'two kilogrammes fruit'.

....
....
....
....
....

4 Wo gehst du gern einkaufen?

- Using compound nouns and plurals of nouns
- H Using dual-case prepositions followed by the dative

1 Unjumble the letters to find the German adjectives. Then translate them into English.

1 gillib ....

2 tunb ....

3 rogß ....

4 nielk ....

5 zruk ....

6 galn ....

7 eun ....

8 eteur ....

9 bqueme ....

10 tla ....

2 Work out the meaning of these compound nouns.

1 das Einkaufszentrum ....

2 das Kleidungsgeschäft ....

3 der Supermarkt ....

4 der Buchladen ....

5 das Schuhgeschäft ....

6 die Schreibwaren ....

H 7 das Butterbrot ....

G

In German you can combine two or more words to make a new noun. These are known as **compound nouns**. Sometimes extra letters may be added to make pronunciation easier.

It's useful to work out the meaning of each part of the compound noun as this helps to work out the meaning of the whole word.

3 Complete these German translations with the correct plural noun.

1 Some shops are very expensive.

Einige .... sind sehr teuer.

2 I like these socks.

Mir gefallen diese ....

3 I can pay for the jumpers automatically.

Ich kann automatisch für die .... bezahlen.

4 The shoes fit you well.

Die .... passen dir gut.

5 Someone is opening many cafes.

Jemand eröffnet viele ....

6 You get better prices at the supermarket.

Im Supermarkt bekommt man bessere ....

G

There are different ways of making nouns **plural** in German. You can follow patterns to work out how to form the plurals of different nouns.

	singular	plural
(-e)	Geschäft	Geschäfte
(¨e)	Supermarkt	Supermärkte
(-n)	Straße	Straßen
(-en)	Uhr	Uhren
(-)	Pullover	Pullover
(-er)	Kind	Kinder
(¨er)	Krankenhaus	Krankenhäuser
(-s)	Hotel	Hotels

H 7 You can buy medicines at the pharmacy.

In der Apotheke kann man .... kaufen.

H 8 There are two bakeries where you can buy good bread.

Es gibt zwei ...., wo man gutes Brot kaufen kann.

Use the glossary to look up any words that are unfamiliar on this page, and try to learn them.

F 4 Translate these sentences into German.

1 I like going shopping. ....

2 There are lovely jumpers in the clothes shop. ....

3 You can save money online. ....

4 Someone needs new socks. ....

5 On Saturday I bought some new shoes. ....

H 5 Circle the correct article to complete each sentence. Then translate the sentences into English.

1 Meine Socken sind unter **dem / der / den** Tisch (*m*). ....

....

2 Ich habe die App auf **meinem / meiner / meinen** Handy (*nt*). ....

....

3 Über **dem / der / den** Kleidung (*f*) steht die Marke. ....

....

4 Das Einkaufszentrum befindet sich zwischen **dem / der / den** Apotheke (*f*) und **dem / der / den** Käsegeschäft (*nt*). ....

....

5 Ich stelle den Stuhl neben **das / dem / den** Bett (*m*). ....

....

6 Der Stoff liegt hinter **dem / der / den** Bett (*m*). ....

....

7 In **diesem / dieser / diesen** Geschäft (*m*) verkauft man leckere Butterbrote. ....

....

8 Ich lege meine Kleidung auf **den / die / dem** Stuhl (*m*). ....

....

G

H Dual-case prepositions can be followed by the **accusative** if movement is implied or by the **dative** if no movement is implied.

an on (the wall)
auf on (the bed)
hinter behind
in in
neben next to
über over
unter under
vor in front of
zwischen between

H 6 Translate this paragraph into English on a separate sheet.

Im Käsegeschäft riecht es nach Käse, aber für mich ist das wirklich kein Problem. In der Bäckerei, wo ich gern Brot kaufe, sind die Preise ziemlich gut. Am Wochenende hat meine Mutter im Einkaufszentrum für uns neue Kleidung und Socken gekauft. Mein Bruder trägt gern Markenschuhe, obwohl sie teuer sind.

5 Mein idealer Wohnort

F Using a range of tenses • F Using *ich möchte*

1 Draw lines to match up the German with the English nouns.

1 der Baum	**a** town
2 die Küste	**b** house
3 die Wohnung	**c** tree
4 das Haus	**d** village
5 das Dorf	**e** coast
6 die Stadt	**f** gym
7 die Pflanze	**g** flat
8 das Fitnesszentrum	**h** plant

2 Complete these sentences with the correct imperfect tense form of the verb in brackets.

1 Ich .... eine kleine Wohnung. (*haben*)

2 Ich .... sehr glücklich. (*sein*)

3 Er .... dieses Haus. (*wollen*)

4 Ich .... in einem großen Haus wohnen. (*wollen*)

5 Es .... viele Bäume. (*geben*)

6 Wir .... eine moderne Wohnung. (*haben*)

G

The **perfect tense** is used in spoken German and in more informal writing.
Ich habe in der Schweiz gewohnt.
I lived in Switzerland.
The **imperfect tense** is used in written narrative accounts, stories and reviews.
ich war I was
ich hatte I had
es gab there was/were
Look back at page 62 of this workbook for a reminder of modal verbs in the imperfect tense.

3 Underline the verbs in each sentence. Then translate the verbal phrases into English.

1 Ich möchte im Ausland wohnen. ....

2 Ich möchte eine Aktivität machen. ....

3 Ich möchte in ein Dorf gehen. ....

4 Ich möchte an der Küste leben. ....

G

To say what you **would like** to do, use *möchte* with a second verb (infinitive) at the end of the sentence.
Ich ***möchte*** *in einer Wohnung* ***wohnen***.
I **would like to live** in an apartment.

4 Translate these sentences into English.

1 Ich wohne in einer modernen Wohnung. ....

2 Ich lebe gern hier, weil es sehr grün ist. ....

....

3 Ich habe nicht gern in einem Dorf gewohnt, denn es war sehr langweilig. ....

....

4 Als ich jünger war, habe ich in einer Stadt gewohnt. ....

....

5 Ich möchte in Deutschland leben. ....

5 Mein idealer Wohnort (1)

H Using regular verbs in the imperfect tense

H 1 Complete these sentences by translating the word in brackets into German.

1 Es gibt viele kulturelle .... (*activities*) für junge Leute.

2 Es gibt einige .... (*trees*).

3 Es gibt bunte .... (*plants*) im Garten.

4 In der Schweiz gibt es viele schöne .... (*towns*).

5 Die .... (*apartments*) sind sehr groß.

6 Die .... (*houses*) sind sehr modern.

G

H The **imperfect tense** is used mainly in written narrative accounts and stories to describe an event in the past.

For regular verbs in the imperfect tense, form the stem by removing *-en* from the end of the infinitive, then add the imperfect tense endings.

When a verb stem ends in *-t*, just remove *-n*:

*war**ten** → war**te**- → ich war**tete***

Depending on the context, the imperfect tense can be translated in different ways:

Ich lernte Deutsch. I learned German. / I used to learn German. / I was learning German.

ich	mach**te**
du	mach**test**
er/sie/es/man	mach**te**
wir	mach**ten**
ihr	mach**tet**
Sie	mach**ten**
sie	mach**ten**

H 2 Rewrite these sentences on a separate sheet, putting the verb into the imperfect tense.

1 In meinem Zimmer tanze ich.

2 Ich spiele Handball.

3 Er macht die Aufgabe.

4 Du kaufst oft Bücher.

5 Er hört nicht gern Musik.

6 Wir arbeiten im Haus.

H 3 Complete these German translations by putting the verbs in brackets into the correct form of the imperfect tense.

1 I asked my mum. — *Ich .... (fragen) meine Mutter.*

2 He often laughed. — *Er.. (lachen) oft.*

3 She loved the book. — *Sie.. (lieben) das Buch.*

4 We hated the school. — *Wir.. (hassen) die Schule.*

5 I worked in an office. — *Ich.. (arbeiten) in einem Büro.*

6 He said 'yes'. — *Er.. (sagen) „Ja".*

7 Did you want to meet somebody? — *.. (Wollen) du jemanden treffen?*

H 4 Translate these sentences into German on a separate sheet.

1 I used to dance at school.

2 I loved the film because it was exciting.

3 She often bought clothes.

4 We always asked the teacher.

5 They loved the series although it was very long.

5 Mein idealer Wohnort (2)

H Using irregular verbs in the imperfect tense

H 1 These imperfect tense verbs are all in the *ich, er/sie/es/man* forms. Draw lines to match them up with their infinitives. Then translate the imperfect tense verbs into English.

1 fiel	**a** sitzen
2 ließ	**b** lassen
3 rief	**c** trinken
4 saß	**d** fallen
5 trank	**e** scheinen
6 schien	**f** rufen
7 warf	**g** verschwinden
8 verschwand	**h** werfen

G

H Many verbs are irregular in the imperfect tense.

	infinitive	**imperfect tense (*ich, er/sie/es/man* forms)**
to bring	bringen	brachte
to think	denken	dachte
to eat	essen	aß
to go (in a vehicle)	fahren	fuhr
to happen	geschehen	geschah
to take	nehmen	nahm
to see	sehen	sah

The *wir/Sie/sie* forms take -(*e*)*n*, e.g. *wir sahen*.

H 2 Circle all the imperfect tense verbs in this text. List them and translate them into English on a separate sheet.

laut *according to*
zunehmen *to increase*

There are 16 imperfect tense verbs in the text in exercise 2.
Look out for common irregular verbs that may be familiar to you:
haben → hatte *sein → war*
gehen → ging *finden → fand*

You may also spot imperfect tense forms of these verbs:
anfangen *kommen*
bleiben *mögen*
kennen *schreiben*

Als ich jünger war, wohnte ich in einer Kleinstadt. Die Bevölkerung da nahm immer zu, aber laut meiner Mutter blieb die Stadt sehr ruhig. Mit sechs Jahren fing ich an, in die Schule zu gehen. Ich mochte es sehr und ging jeden Tag zu Fuß dorthin. Im Großen und Ganzen dachte ich, dass die Schule sehr gut war. Ich kannte ein bisschen Deutsch, weil unser Lehrer aus Deutschland kam. Ich sprach Englisch und Türkisch zu Hause, aber ich schrieb nur Englisch. Meine Mutter half mir, wenn ich Englischhausaufgaben hatte, weil ich das schwierig fand.

H 3 Complete the English translations.

1 Ich nahm das Buch mit.	*I .... the book with me.*
2 Das Geschäft schloss um sechs Uhr.	*The shop .... at 6 o'clock.*
3 Der Stuhl stand neben dem Bett.	*The chair .... next to the bed.*
4 Er stieg die Treppe hoch.	*He .... up the stairs.*
5 Wir verstanden Deutsch.	*We .... German.*
6 Sie wusste das schon.	*She already .... that.*
7 Er gab ihr das Kleingeld.	*He .... her the change.*

H 4 Translate these sentences into German on a separate sheet, using the imperfect tense.

1 I fell on the mountain.

2 The film started at 6 o'clock.

3 She helped her father with the housework.

4 You liked the series because it was funny.

5 Afterwards he disappeared.

6 The accident happened behind the house.

5 Mein idealer Wohnort (3)

H Revising the conditional

H 1 Translate these sentences into English.

> **G** H You can use the imperfect subjunctive form of *mögen* to say 'would like'.
> *Ich* ***möchte*** *eine Jacke.*
> I would like a jacket.
> *Ich* ***möchte*** *eine Jacke* ***kaufen****.*
> I would like to buy a jacket.

1 Ich möchte in die Stadtmitte gehen.

....

2 Möchtest du ins Geschäft gehen?

....

3 Er möchte Zeit sparen. ....

4 Sie möchte die Ware verkaufen. ....

5 Wir möchten die Kleidung anprobieren. ....

6 Sie möchten Butterbrote essen. ....

H 2 Complete each German translation with the missing verb.

> **G** H To form the conditional, use würde with an **infinitive**:
> *Ich würde* ***tanzen****.* I would dance.
> *Er würde das Haus* ***verlassen****.*
> He would leave the house.
> Use *würde* with *gern* to mean 'would like':
> *Ich* ***würde gern*** *in Deutschland leben.*
> I would like to live in Germany.
> In Module 4, you met **wäre** and **hätte** in sentences like these:
> *Wenn ich müde wäre, würde ich schlafen.*
> If I were tired, I would sleep.
> *Wenn ich Hunger hätte, würde ich essen.*
> If I were hungry, I would eat.
> ***wäre*** can also mean 'would be':
> *Es* ***wäre*** *modern.* It would be modern.
> ***hätte*** can also mean 'would have':
> *Es* ***hätte*** *drei Schlafzimmer.*
> It would have three bedrooms.
> Note also: ***Es gäbe*** *einen Garten.*
> **There would be** a garden.

1 *The garden would be very lovely.*

Der Garten .... sehr schön.

2 *The town would have many trees and plants.*

Die Stadt .... viele Bäume und Pflanzen.

3 *I would like to live in Austria.*

Ich .... gern in Österreich leben.

4 *I would like a horse.*

Ich .... gern ein Pferd.

5 *My dad would be very angry.*

Mein Vater .... sehr böse.

6 *We would like to move to a new house.*

Wir .... gern in ein neues Haus ziehen.

H 3 Translate these sentences into English.

1 Ich würde gern ins Fitnesszentrum gehen. ....

2 Er würde eine Fahrkarte kaufen. ....

3 Die Waren würden direkt nach Hause kommen. ....

4 Der Stoff wäre sehr schön. ....

5 Es gäbe viele Socken. ....

6 Sie würde ein neues Geschäft eröffnen. ....

H 4 Translate this paragraph into German on a separate sheet.

When I was younger, I lived in a village. According to my grandma it was very lovely but there were not many activities. In the future I would like to live in a town. It would be quite big, and it would have a good shop, a park and a café.

6 Bei mir zu Hause

- Using prepositions with the accusative and the dative
- Working out the meaning of compound nouns

1 Use your knowledge of compound nouns to work out the meanings of these rooms of the house.

1 die Essecke ....

2 das Arbeitszimmer ....

3 das Schlafzimmer ....

4 das Wohnzimmer ....

5 das Badezimmer ....

6 das Esszimmer ....

G German often combines two or more words to make new nouns. These are called **compound nouns**. They combine two nouns, a verb stem and a noun, or an adjective and a noun.

2 Draw lines to match up the sentences with the rooms.

1 Hier esse ich.	a das Badezimmer
2 Hier arbeite ich.	b das Büro
3 Hier spiele ich Fußball.	c das Wohnzimmer
4 Hier nehme ich ein Bad.	d das Esszimmer
5 Hier sehe ich fern.	e die Küche
6 Hier koche ich.	f der Garten
H 7 Es schützt das ganze Haus!	g das Dach

G Some **prepositions** are followed by the **accusative** when there is movement towards an object and the **dative** if there is no movement towards an object.

an on (the wall)
auf on (the bed)
in in

H
hinter behind
neben next to
über over
unter under
vor in front of
zwischen between

Wir stellen die Pflanze ***auf den*** *Tisch.* We are putting the plant on the table.
Die Pflanze ist ***auf dem*** *Tisch.* The plant is on the table.

3 Underline the preposition in each sentence. Decide if there is movement towards an object or no movement towards an object and write down the case used after the preposition: accusative or dative.

1 Ich lege die Jacke auf das Bett. ....

2 Der Tisch kommt ins Haus. ....

3 Das Buch ist in der Tasche. ....

4 Wir stellen den Stuhl auf den Boden. ....

H 5 Die Wohnung liegt im ersten Stock. ....

H 6 Es gibt eine Wand zwischen der Küche und dem Esszimmer. ....

Some prepositions and definite articles are shortened into one word:
an + das → ans
auf + das → aufs
in + das → ins
in + dem → im

4 Complete these sentences with the correct form of the definite article.

1 Ich schlafe in .... Schlafzimmer (*nt*).

2 Er geht in .... Wohnzimmer (*nt*).

3 Die Jacke ist an .... Tür (*f*).

H 4 Ich stelle den Tisch neben .... Essecke (*f*).

H 5 Wir stellen den Stuhl vor .... Tisch (*m*).

H 6 Wir sind in .... neue Haus (*nt*) gezogen.

H 5 Rewrite each sentence, putting the words into the correct order. Start with the 'place' element.

1 ich Hier koche ....

2 es gibt Unten Zimmer zwei ....

3 es Hinten gibt Mauer eine ....

4 Oben Schlafzimmer es gibt vier ....

5 fern sehe Wohnzimmer Im ich ....

6 Garten spiele Tennis ich mit Bruder meinem Im ....

> **G**
> The verb is always the second idea of a German sentence. This means if something else comes first, then the **verb** and the subject must swap over.
> *Unten **gibt** es vier Zimmer.*
> Downstairs there are four rooms.
> *Hinten **gibt** es einen Garten.*
> Behind there is a garden.
> *Oben **gibt** es drei Schlafzimmer.*
> Upstairs there are three bedrooms.

F 6 Translate these sentences into German.

1 I work in the office. ....

2 I like living here because the house is lovely. ....

3 I sleep in the big bedroom. ....

4 The garden is fifty metres long. ....

5 Yesterday I worked in the kitchen. ....

H 7 Translate this paragraph into English.

Gestern bin ich in das neue Haus im Norden gezogen. Unten haben wir vier Zimmer und oben im ersten Stock haben wir vier Zimmer. Wir haben den Tisch und vier Stühle in die Küche gestellt. An den Wänden haben wir neue Bilder, aber wir haben unsere alten Fotos unter das Bett gesteckt!

....

Glossary

bold = this word will appear in Higher exams only

ab	*from, as of*
als	*than, when, as*
am	*on, at the (m, nt) (dative) /* ***in the process of, during, while***
ans	*on(to) the, at the (nt) (accusative)*
Apotheke (f)	*pharmacy, chemist's*
App (f)	*app*
(Arnzei)mittel (nt)	*medicine*
aß	*(I/she, he, it) ate*
auf	*on, onto, at, to*
aus	*out, out of, from*
Ausland (nt)	*abroad*
außer	*except*
Auto (nt)	*car*
automatisch	*automatic, automatically*
Bäckerei (f)	*bakery*
Bahn (f)	*railway*
Bahnhof (m)	*station*
Bank (f)	*bank, bench*
bei	*at (the house of), with /* ***in the process of, during, while***
beim	*at (the house of) the (m, nt) /* ***in the process of, during, while***
Bereich (m)	*area*
Bevölkerung (f)	*population*
bis	*until, till, up to*
blieb	*(I/she, he, it) remained, stayed*
Boden (m)	*floor, ground*
Boot (nt)	*boat*
brachte	*(I/she, he, it) brought*
breit	*broad, broadly*
Brücke (f)	*bridge*
Büro (nt)	*office*
Bus (m)	*bus*
Busse (pl)	*buses*
Butterbrot (nt)	*piece of bread (with butter), sandwich*
Dach (nt)	*roof*
dachte	*(I/she, he, it) thought*
der/die/das meiste ...	*the most ...*
direkt	*direct, directly, straight*
Dorf (nt)	*village*
durch	*through,* ***by***
Ecke (f)	*corner*
einige	*a few, some*
Einkaufszentrum (nt)	*shopping centre*
Einwohner (m)	*inhabitant, resident*
einzig	*only, single*
eng	*narrow, narrowly, close, closely, tight (clothing)*
entfernt	*away, distant*
entlang	*along*
Entschuldigung	*excuse me*
eröffnen	*(to) open, start | opening, starting*
erreichen	*(to) reach, catch (the bus) | reaching, catching*
(der/die/eine) Erwachsene (m/f), (ein) Erwachsener (m), Erwachsene (pl), (die) Erwachsenen (pl)	*adult, the adults*

Fahrkarte (f)	*ticket*			
Fahrrad/Rad (nt)	*bicycle, bike*			
fährst	*(you (sing informal)) go (by transport), drive, travel*			
Fahrt (f)	*journey, trip*			
Fahrzeug (nt)	*vehicle*			
Feld (nt)	*field*			
fern	*far, distant*			
fiel	*(I/she, he, it) fell*			
fing ... an	*(I/she, he, it) started*			
fliegen	*(to) fly | flying*			
Flughafen (m)	*airport*			
Flugzeug (nt)	*plane, aeroplane*			
Franken (m)	*(Swiss) franc*			
frisch	*fresh, freshly*			
fuhr	*(I/she, he, it) went (by transport), drove*			
führen	*(to) lead, guide | leading, guiding*			
für	*for*			
gab	*(I/she, he, it) gave*			
Garten (m)	*garden*			
gefällt	*(she, he, it, one) pleases | is pleasing*			
gegen	*against*			
Gegend (f)	*area*			
gegenüber	*opposite*			
generell	*generally*			
geradeaus	*straight on*			
Geschäft (nt)	*shop, business, trade*			
geschah	*(I/she, he, it) happened*			
geschehen	*(to) happen | happening*			
(aux) ... gezogen	*pulled, moved / (have, has) pulled, moved*			
ging	*(I/she, he, it) went, walked*			
Größe (f)	*height, size*			
half	*(I/she, he, it) helped*			
Hauptstadt (f)	*capital city*			
Haus (nt)	*house*			
Heimat (f)	*homeland, home country*			
her	*from something, in this direction*			
hinten	*at the back*			
hinter	*behind*			
hoch	*high, tall*			
Höhe (f)	*height, hill*			
im	*in the (m, nt) (dative)*			
im Großen und Ganzen	*by and large, in general*			
in	*in, into*			
in der Nähe (von)	*nearby, near*			
ins	*into the (nt) (accusative)*			
jemand	*someone (subj)*			
jemanden	*someone (obj)*			
jung	*young*			
kälter	*colder*			
kam	*(I/she, he, it) came*			
kannte	*(I/she, he, it) knew*			
Kasse (f)	*checkout, till*			
Kilo(gramm) (nt)	*kilo(gram)*			
Kleidung (f)	*clothing*			
Kleingeld (nt)	*change (money)*			
kommen	*(to) come | coming*			
kosten	*(to) cost | costing*			
Kosten (pl)	*costs*			
kulturell	*cultural, culturally*			
Laden (m)	*shop*			
Ladung (f)	*charge, load*			
Lage (f)	*situation, location*			

Land (nt); aufs / auf dem Land	*country, land, state; countryside*			
länger	*longer*			
laut (prep)	*according to*			
leben	*(to) live | living*			
ließ	*(I/she, he, it) let, allowed, left*			
link-	*left*			
links	*to/on the left*			
Marke (f)	*brand*			
Mauer (f)	*wall*			
Meter (m)	*metre*			
mit	*with*			
mitnehmen	*(to) take/bring along | taking/bringing along*			
Mitte (f)	*middle, centre*			
mochte	*(I/she, he, it, one) liked*			
mochtest	*(you (sing informal)) liked*			
multikulturell	*multicultural*			
nach	*to, towards, after, according to*			
Nachbar (m)	*neighbour*			
nah	*near, nearby, close*			
nahm	*(I/she, he, it) took*			
national	*national, nationally*			
neben	*next to, beside*			
niedrig	*low*			
Norden (m)	*north*			
offen	*open, openly*			
öffentlich	*public, municipal*			
Öffentlichkeit (f)	*public*			
Osten (m)	*east*			
passen	*(to) fit, suit | fitting, suiting*			
Pflanze (f)	*plant*			
Post (f)	*post office*			
Preis (m)	*price, prize*			
privat	*(in) private, privately*			
pro	*by, per*			
Rand (m)	*edge*			
recht-	*right*			
rechts	*on/to the right*			
Richtung (f)	*direction*			
riechen	*(to) smell | smelling*			
rief	*(I/she, he, it) called, shouted*			
Rückfahrkarte (f)	*return ticket*			
sah	*(I/she, he, it) saw*			
saß/sass	*(I/she, he, it) sat*			
schien	*(I/she, he, it) shone, seemed, appeared*			
Schiff (nt)	*ship, boat*			
schloss	*(I/she, he, it) closed, shut*			
schrieb	*(I/she, he, it) wrote*			
sich befinden	*(to) be (situated) | being (situated)*			
Socke (f)	*sock*			
sollen	*(to) ought to, be supposed to, should*			
sparen	*(to) save (e.g. money) | saving (e.g. money)*			
sprach	*(I/she, he, it) spoke*			
Sprache (f)	*language*			
Stadion (nt)	*stadium*			
Stadt (f)	*town, city*			
stand	*(I/she, he, it) stood*			
stecken	*(to) put (in) | putting (in)*			
stellen	*(to) put, place | putting, placing*			
stieg	*(I/she, he, it) increased, climbed*			

Stock (m)	*floor (e.g. of a hotel), storey*
Stoff (m)	*material, fabric*
Straßenbahn (f)	*tram*
Straßenplan (m)	*map (street)*
Strecke (f)	*distance, route*
Supermarkt (m)	*supermarket*
Süden (m)	*south*
Tasche (f)	*bag, pocket*
tot	*dead*
trank	*(I/she, he, it) drank*
Treppe (f)	*stairs, staircase*
U-Bahn (f)	*underground train*
über	*above, over, about, through*
um	***around**, at (+ time)*
Umgebung (f)	*surroundings*
unten	*below, downstairs*
unter	*under, below, among*
verkaufen	*(to) sell | selling*
Verkehr (m)	*traffic*
verschwand	*(I/she, he, it) disappeared*
verstand	*(I/she, he, it, one) understood*
vom	*from the, of the (m, nt)*
von	*from, of*
vor	*in front of, before, ago*
Wagen (m)	*car, carriage*
Wand (f)	*wall*
Ware (f)	*goods*
warf	*(I/she, he, it) threw*
weißt	*(you (sing informal)) know (something)*
weitergehen	*(to) continue, go on | continuing, going on*
Westen (m)	*west*
wissen	*(to) know (something) | knowing (something) | (we/they/you (formal)) know (something)*
woher	*where … from?*
wohnen	*(to) live, stay | living, staying*
Wohnung (f)	*flat, apartment*
wolltest	*(you (sing informal)) wanted (to)*
wusste	*(I/she, he, it) knew*
Zeichen (nt)	*sign*
zentral	*central, centrally*
ziehen	*(to) pull, move | pulling, moving*
zu	*to*
Zug (m)	*train*
zum, zur	*to the (m, nt), to the (f), about, for*
zunehmen	*(to) increase | increasing*
zurück	*back*
zwischen	*between*

Foundation translation revision

German to English

1 Circle the odd one out.

1 Pulli / T-Shirt / Schuhe / Hose

2 Montag / Mathe / Kunst / Englisch

3 Smartphone / Bilder / Handy / Telefon

4 Tante / Onkel / Schwester / Stiefmutter

5 Brot / Wasser / Obst / Gemüse

2 Draw lines to match up the German sentences with their English translations.

1 In der Schule mache ich Sport.

2 In meiner Freizeit höre ich manchmal Musik.

3 Ich verstehe mich gar nicht gut mit meinem Bruder, der sehr laut ist.

4 Ich schlafe nicht genug, weil ich zu spät ins Bett gehe.

5 Letztes Wochenende habe ich im Kleidungsgeschäft einen neuen Pulli gekauft.

a In my free time I sometimes listen to music.

b I don't sleep enough because I go to bed too late.

c At school I do sport.

d Last weekend I bought a new jumper in the clothes shop.

e I don't get on at all well with my brother, who is very loud.

3 Complete these sentences by translating the words in brackets into English.

1 .... (*Am Montag*) in the first lesson I have .... (*Musik*).

2 In .... (*meiner Freizeit*) I often stream .... (*Videos*).

3 I .... (*verstehe mich ziemlich gut*) with my mum, who is very .... (*ruhig*).

4 I .... (*verbringe*) too much time on my .... (*Handy*).

5 .... (*Am Wochenende*) I bought .... (*ein Geschenk*) in the souvenir shop.

4 Translate these sentences into English.

1 In der Schule lerne ich Mathe. ....

2 In meiner Freizeit sehe ich oft Filme. ....

3 Ich verstehe mich gut mit meiner Freundin, die sehr nett ist.

....

4 Ich esse ungesund, weil ich viel Schokolade mag.

....

5 Gestern habe ich im Schuhgeschäft neue Schuhe gekauft.

....

English to German

1 Match up the English words with their German translations. Write the correct letter.

1 school uniform .....
2 swimming .....
3 programmes .....
4 stepfather .....
5 walking .....

a die Sendungen
b das Spazierengehen
c das Schwimmen
d der Stiefvater
e die Schuluniform

2 Complete each German translation using a word from the box.

Komödien Woche laufen Bibliothek spazieren

1 I go walking very often.	*Ich gehe sehr oft ....*
2 I think that the library is too quiet.	*Ich finde die .... zu leise.*
3 I like comedies because they're really funny.	*Ich mag ...., denn sie sind wirklich lustig.*
4 At the weekend I will go running in the park.	*Ich werde am Wochenende im Park .... gehen.*
5 Last week I went to a big party.	*Letzte .... bin ich auf eine große Party gegangen.*

3 Circle the correct option to complete each German translation.

1 I ride my bike three times a week.	*Ich fahre* ***manchmal / dreimal pro Woche*** *Rad.*
2 I find this rule quite right.	*Ich finde diese Regel ganz* ***wichtig / richtig****.*
3 I dislike documentaries because they're quite boring.	*Ich mag Dokumentarfilme nicht, weil sie ganz* ***langweilig / toll*** *sind.*
4 I will play football in the park with my friend later.	*Ich werde später mit meiner Freundin im Park* ***Handball / Fußball*** *spielen.*
5 Last month we celebrated my birthday.	***Letzte Woche / Letzten Monat*** *haben wir meinen Geburtstag gefeiert.*

4 Translate these sentences into German.

1 I play tennis twice a week.

....

2 I think that the school rules are impractical.

....

3 I like adventure films because they are particularly exciting.

....

4 At the weekend I will go shopping with my friend in the town centre.

....

5 Last year we celebrated carnival in Cologne.

....

Higher translation revision

German to English

1 Circle the odd one out.

1 Direktor / Lehrer / Schauspieler / Schüler
2 richtig / schön / praktisch / unbequem
3 Krimi / Ausstellung / Komödie / Film
4 Bildschirm / Handy / Smartphone / Vorstellung
5 Eigenschaft / Kontakt / Verständnis / Beziehung

2 Draw lines to match up the German sentences with their English translations.

1 Ich finde diese Regel nicht wichtig.
2 Ich sehe ab und zu Filme, denn die Geschichten sind interessant.
3 Ich bin nicht in Form, weil ich mich nicht genug bewege.
4 Ich habe schlechte Beziehungen zu meinen Eltern.
5 Letztes Wochenende haben wir im Garten zusammen gegessen.

a I have bad relationships with my parents.
b I watch films now and again because the stories are interesting.
c Last weekend we ate in the garden together.
d I find this rule unimportant.
e I'm not fit because I don't exercise enough.

3 Correct the English translation by crossing through the incorrect word(s) and writing the correction above it.

Ich mag meine Schule nicht. Ich bin der Meinung, dass die Schulregeln falsch sind. Zu Hause streame ich oft Horrorfilme, denn es gibt in diesen Filmen viel Spannung. Ich verbringe zu viel Zeit mit meinen Freunden, obwohl ich mich gut mit meinen Schwestern verstehe. Letzten Sommer sind wir alle zusammen zum Strand gegangen.

I like my school. I'm of the opinion that the school rules are right. At home I often stream horrible videos because there is a lot of atmosphere in these videos. I spend too little time with my friend, although I don't get on well with my sisters. Last autumn we all went to the lake together.

4 Translate this paragraph into English.

Ich mag meine Schule und ich finde den Direktor sehr freundlich. Zu Hause sehe ich häufig Serien an, denn die Schauspieler sind sehr gut. Ich sitze in meinem Zimmer zu viel vor dem Bildschirm, obwohl ich auch gern Sport mit meinen Eltern treibe. Am Wochenende sind wir im Park spazieren gegangen.

English to German

1 Draw lines to match up the English with the German words.

1 atmosphere
2 exercise
3 exhibition
4 club
5 performance

a die Vorstellung
b die Ausstellung
c der Verein
d die Stimmung
e die Aufgabe

2 Complete each German translation using a word from the box.

konnte angesehen
spielen gab
heruntergeladen

1 *Yesterday I downloaded photos from social media.* — Gestern habe ich Fotos von sozialen Medien ....
2 *Last weekend I watched a series which was very funny.* — Letztes Wochenende habe ich eine Serie ...., die sehr lustig war.
3 *In the film there was a lot of tension.* — Im Film .... es viel Spannung.
4 *I couldn't work because I was very tired.* — Ich .... nicht arbeiten, weil ich sehr müde war.
5 *Tomorrow I will go to the tennis club and play with my friends.* — Morgen werde ich zum Tennisverein gehen und mit meinen Freunden ....

3 Circle the correct option to complete each German translation.

1 *Yesterday I had lots of work.* — **Gestern hatte ich** / **Heute habe ich** viel Arbeit.
2 *The work was very difficult.* — Die Arbeit war sehr **leicht** / **schwierig**.
3 *I couldn't work.* — Ich **kannte** / **konnte** nicht arbeiten.
4 *I downloaded some photos.* — Ich habe einige **Freunde eingeladen** / **Fotos heruntergeladen**.
5 *We are preparing an exhibition.* — Wir bereiten eine **Vorstellung** / **Ausstellung** vor.

4 Translate this paragraph into German.

Yesterday I had lots of homework and the exercises were very difficult. I couldn't concentrate very well. Afterwards I downloaded a film which I watched on the computer. The film had a good atmosphere but there was violence. Tonight I will go to theatre club because we are preparing a performance.

....

....

....

....

....

....

Kulturzone Im Urlaub und unterwegs

F Using adjectival endings after the definite article

1 Tick the correct translation: a or b.

1 landen
- **a** to land ☐
- **b** to travel ☐

2 lassen
- **a** to eat ☐
- **b** to leave ☐

3 mögen
- **a** to like ☐
- **b** to do ☐

4 besuchen
- **a** to see ☐
- **b** to visit ☐

5 antworten
- **a** to become ☐
- **b** to answer ☐

6 kennenlernen
- **a** to get to meet ☐
- **b** to get to know ☐

G

Adjective endings change after the definite article according to the case.

	nominative endings	accusative endings
masculine	**Der** lang**e** Fluss ist der Rhein.	Ich sehe **den** lang**en** Fluss.
feminine	**Die** ganz**e** Welt kommt nach Deutschland.	Ich reise um **die** ganz**e** Welt.
neuter	**Das** interessant**e** Schloss ist in der Nähe von Berlin.	Es gibt **das** interessant**e** Schloss.
plural	**Die** traditionell**en** Besucher kommen aus der Schweiz.	Es gibt **die** traditionell**en** Besucher.

The adjective endings don't change the meaning! *Lang*, *lange* and *langen* all translate as 'long'.

2 Circle the adjective in each sentence. Write which case the adjective is in (nom/acc) and translate it into English.

The adjective *hoh-* is a form of *hoch*. Can you remember what this adjective means?

1. Das hohe Schloss befindet sich auf einem Berg. ....
2. Der dichte Wald ist nicht weit von der Stadt. ....
3. Ich gehe durch den heißen Sand. ....
4. Der lange Fluss geht durch den Wald. ....
5. Die traditionellen Touristen kommen aus Deutschland. ....
6. Wir nehmen die weiße Linie. ....

3 Complete these sentences with the correct form of the adjective in brackets.

1. Ich besuche das .... Schloss. (*historisch*)
2. Die .... Urlaubswohnung ist in Deutschland. (*bequem*)
3. Die .... Besucher kommen im Juli an. (*lokal*)
4. Sie gehen in die .... Cafés. (*beliebt*)
5. Wir sehen den .... See. (*blau*)
6. Der .... Berg heißt das Matterhorn. (*hoch*)

4 Translate these sentences into German on a separate sheet.

1. I like visiting the castle.
2. The interesting museum is in the town centre.
3. We can try the delicious food.
4. I visit the historical towns because they're wonderful.
5. Yesterday I went to the river.

Kulturzone Im Urlaub und unterwegs

H Forming the imperative

H 1 Complete the sentences to match the English translations, using the words in the box.

halten Berliner Eindruck unglaublich riesig Magst zahlreiche ehemalige

1 Die Windkraft ist	*Wind power is incredible.*
2 .... du die traditionelle Küche?	*Do you like traditional cuisine?*
3 Der Zug wird im Dorf	*The train will stop in the village.*
4 Er ist	*He is from Berlin.*
5 Es gibt .... historische Orte, die ich besuchen möchte.	*There are numerous historical places that I would like to visit.*
6 Der Berg ist .... hoch.	*The mountain is hugely high.*
7 Das .... Museum ist ein Gebäude aus dem letzten Jahrhundert.	*The former museum is a building from the last century.*
8 Die schöne Landschaft macht einen wunderbaren	*The beautiful landscape makes a wonderful impression.*

G

H Use the **imperative** form to give instructions.
In a **formal** situation:
***Beantworten Sie** die Frage!*
In an **informal** situation:
***Mach** die Hausaufgaben!* (*du* form)
***Macht** die Hausaufgaben!* (*ihr* form)

sein has an irregular imperative form:
Sie: ***Seien** Sie klar!* Be clear!
ihr: ***Seid** leise!* Be quiet!
du: **Sei** *laut!* Be loud!

H 2 Draw lines to match up the pairs of sentences.

1 Was für ein Geräusch ist das?	**a** Macht einen Kurs!
2 Magst du Schwimmen?	**b** Seid ruhig!
3 Abfahrt in fünf Minuten!	**c** Geh ins Schwimmbad!
4 Ist das zu teuer für dich?	**d** Kauf das billigste T-Shirt!
5 Wollt ihr Deutsch lernen?	**e** Vergiss nichts!
6 Du lässt immer etwas zu Hause.	**f** Verpassen Sie den Zug nicht!

H 3 Complete these German sentences with the correct imperative form of the verb in brackets.

nennen *to name*

1 .... ruhig! (*Be* – du)

2 .... ein Schloss! (*Build* – ihr)

3 .... eine ermüdende Aktivität! (*Do* – Sie)

4 .... den höchsten Berg! (*Name* – du)

5 .... nicht Ihre liebsten Erinnerungen! (*Forget* – Sie)

6 Am besten .... geradeaus. (*Go* – Sie)

H 4 Translate this text into English on a separate sheet.

Seien Sie ehrlich! Besuchst du gern historische Orte, wie ich? Ich sehe alte Gebäude am liebsten, weil ich sie äußerst interessant finde. Mein Freund ist Berliner und er denkt, dass Deutschland die beliebtesten Museen hat. Meiner Meinung nach hat er bestimmt Recht. Nächsten Sommer werde ich nach Österreich fahren. Ich freue mich darauf!

1 Wo fahren wir hin?

Forming questions • Discussing advantages and disadvantages

1 Draw lines to match up the English with the German words.

1 practical	**a** echt
2 virtual	**b** enorm
3 enormous	**c** günstig
4 quiet	**d** praktisch
5 real/genuine	**e** ruhig
6 wide	**f** virtuell
7 cheap/good	**g** weit

2 Complete these sentences by translating the words in brackets into German.

1 Man muss eine Antwort geben .... (*give*)
2 Ich mag die frische .... (*air*) dict.leo.org.
3 Ich schwimme gern im Meer .... (*sea*) ✓
4 Diese Bahn führt zur Küste .... (*coast*) ✓
5 Diese Übung ist auf einer .... (*page*) im Buch. dict.
6 Ich suche die .... (*tourist information*) dict.
H 7 Man genießt die .... (*silence*)
H 8 Es gibt eine sehr schöne Land — .... (*countryside*)

To form a yes/no question in German, swap over the **subject** and the verb.

***Die Stadt** ist interessant.* → *Ist **die Stadt** interessant?*
The town is interesting. → Is the town interesting?

***Es** gibt viele Städte.* → *Gibt **es** viele Städte?*
There are many towns. → Are there many towns?

G

3 Rewrite each question, putting the words into the correct order. Add a capital letter to the first word.

1 das du Essen magst? Magst du das essen? ✓
2 kauft genug Geschenke er? Kauft er ~~genug~~ Geschenke genug
3 WLAN das sie braucht? Braucht sie das WLAN
4 Touristeninformation es gibt eine? Gibt es Touristeninformation eine
5 mögen Luft wir die frische? Mögen
H 6 besichtigen Sie das wollen Museum? ~~Bes~~ Wollen
H 7 ihr eine möchtet Stadt entdecken andere? Möchtet ihr

4 Complete these German sentences with the correct form of a modal verb and an infinitive from the box.

~~besuchen~~	**H** ~~genießen~~	~~zuhören~~	~~spielen~~	~~schwimmen~~

1 Can you play tennis here? Kann man hier Tennis Spielen?

2 Are you allowed to swim in the sea? .... man im Meer ~~besuchen~~ Schwimmen?

3 Should we visit the old castle? .... man das alte Schloss besuchen?

H 4 You can enjoy the scenery. Man Kann die Landschaft genießen.

H 5 You should listen with attention. Man .... mit Aufmerksamkeit Zuhören.

Use *man* (meaning as 'we', 'you' or 'people') with **modal verbs** to talk about what everyone must, can, should, likes or is allowed to do. The second verb goes to the end of the clause in the infinitive form.
Man ***kann*** *das Geschäft öffnen.* We can open the shop.
Man ***soll*** *die Bank schließen.* We should close the bank.
Man ***darf*** *Aktivitäten anbieten.* We are allowed to offer activities.

H 5 Read this German paragraph and complete the translation into English.

In den Ferien reise ich gern nach Deutschland. Man kann bestimmte Sachen sehen und die alten Gebäude sind echt interessant. Die Landschaft ist sehr schön, mit hohen Bergen und tiefen Seen. Dort muss man schwimmen, um die Seen zu genießen.

In the holidays I **1** like travelling to Germany. You **2** .... see certain things and the old buildings are **3** .... interesting. The countryside is very beautiful with **4** .... mountains and **5** .... lakes. You **6** .... swim there in order to **7** .... the lakes.

F 6 Translate these sentences into English.

1 Ich besuche gern Deutschland. I like to visit Germany

2 Das ist ein sehr schönes Land. ~~Th~~

3 Fährst du gern nach Österreich? Do you like to go to Austria

4 Man kann die alten Schlösser sehen, die wunderbar sind.

....

5 Letzten Sommer habe ich die Schweiz besucht.

Last Summer I visited Switzerland

H 7 Translate this paragraph into German on a separate sheet.

My departure for Switzerland takes place next week. I am going to visit five different cities. I don't know exactly what high mountains there are, but I know there are deep lakes. When I am there, I will do a cookery course. It's quite expensive but the train tickets are cheap.

2 Ich möchte eine Reservierung machen!

Using *wer*, *wen* and *wem* • Recognising negatives

1 Draw lines to match up the German with the English nouns.

1 das Kind	a wife, woman
2 das Bad	b double room
3 das Doppelzimmer	c husband, man
4 das Einzelzimmer	d child
5 die Frau	e single room
6 das Frühstück	f bath/bathroom
7 der Mann	g booking, reservation
8 die Reservierung	h breakfast

2 Complete the sentences using a word from the box.

Zimmer H Vorschlag Region Geld Brief Reise Telefon Details

1 Ich habe einen .... geschrieben.	*I wrote a letter.*
2 Können Sie mir bitte die .... geben?	*Can you give me the details?*
3 Haben Sie ein gute .... gehabt?	*Did you have a good journey?*
4 Haben Sie ein .... frei?	*Do you have a free room?*
5 Mögen Sie diese ....?	*Do you like this region?*
6 Wir haben insgesamt dreimal am .... gesprochen.	*In total we spoke on the telephone three times.*
7 Ich muss .... wechseln.	*I have to change money.*
H 8 Ich habe einen .... für Sie.	*I have a suggestion for you.*

3 Complete these sentences with the correct form of *wer*.

1 .... braucht diese Informationen?

2 Mit .... fahren Sie nach Deutschland?

3 Für .... ist die Reservierung?

4 Bei .... lässt du dein Fahrrad?

5 .... spielt Tennis?

G

wer is an **interrogative** (question word) that changes its form depending on the case:

nominative	***Wer*** *reserviert das Zimmer?* Who is booking the room?
accusative	*Für* ***wen*** *wollen Sie bezahlen?* For whom do you want to pay?
dative	*Mit* ***wem*** *fahren Sie?* With whom are you going?

4 Underline the negative in each sentence. Then translate the sentences into English.

1 Ich verbringe die Ferien nie an der Küste. ....

....

G

Learn to recognise negatives, as these change the meaning of the sentence.

ohne without	*niemand* no-one
kein no, not a	*nichts* nothing
nie never	H *weder ... noch* neither ... nor
nicht not	

2 Es gibt nichts zu tun. ....

3 Ich reise ohne meinen Mann. ....

....

H 4 Niemand möchte das Einzelzimmer oben im Dach. ....

....

H 5 Es gibt keinen Blick aufs Meer. ....

H 6 Frühstück ist nicht inklusive. ....

H 5 Complete these sentences by translating the words in brackets into German.

1 Wir wollen .... (*neither*) in einem Hotel .... (*nor*) in einer Ferienwohnung übernachten.

2 .... (*No one*) kann mit einer Kreditkarte bezahlen.

3 Ich bitte .... (*never*) um Hilfe.

4 Ich fahre .... (*not*) mit dem Boot.

5 Natürlich kann man dort .... (*nothing*) tun.

6 .... (*Without*) wen kommen Sie an?

Look back at exercise 2 for help with unfamiliar vocabulary in exercise 6.

F 6 Translate these sentences into German.

1 I never travel with the school. ....

2 Thank you for your letter. ....

3 In total that costs exactly forty euros. ....

4 That was very expensive. ....

5 I changed sixty euros. ....

H 7 Translate this paragraph into English.

Ich danke Ihnen für den Brief und freue mich auf Ihre Ankunft. Mit wem kommen Sie? Ich habe Zimmer für Sie im Hotel reserviert. Das Einzelzimmer und das Doppelzimmer teilen ein großes Bad. Die Zimmer sind inklusive Frühstück. Es gibt nichts zu tun, aber der Blick ist schön.

....

....

....

....

....

....

3 Probleme, Probleme

Revising possessive adjectives

1 Match up the German words with the pictures. Write the correct letter (a–h).

1 der Koffer ....

2 der Pass ....

3 das Bett ....

4 der Stuhl ....

5 die Straße ....

6 die Tür ....

7 das Fenster ....

H 8 die Kreditkarte ....

a
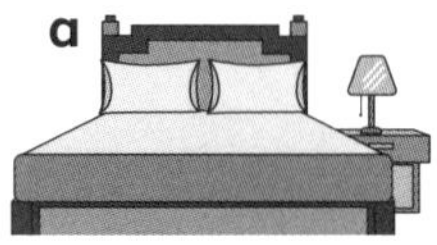

b
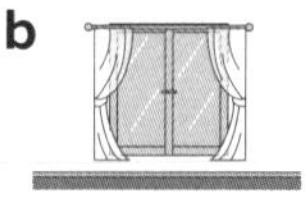

c
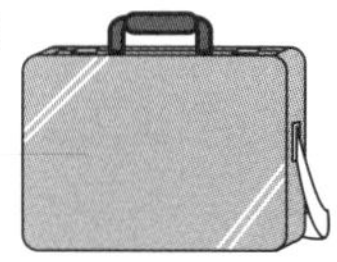

d
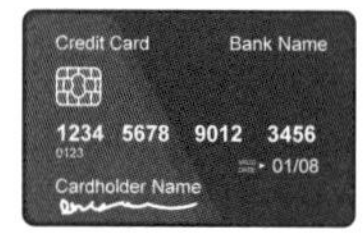

e

f

g

h
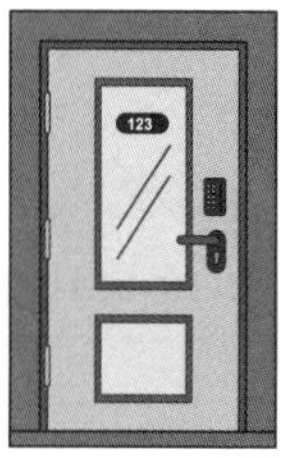

2 Circle the correct option to complete each English translation.

1 Wir haben den Zug verpasst. *We missed the* ***plane*** */* ***train****.*

2 Ich habe das Kleid anprobiert. *I tried on the* ***skirt*** */* ***dress****.*

3 Er hat seinen Pass vergessen. *He forgot his* ***credit card*** */* ***passport****.*

4 Du hältst die Tür offen. *You hold the* ***window*** */* ***door*** *open.*

H 5 Unterwegs habe ich mein Gepäck verloren. *On the way I lost my* ***luggage*** */* ***clothes****.*

H 6 Nur meine Ohrhörer funktionieren nicht. *Only my* ***earbuds*** */* ***speakers*** *don't work.*

H 7 Ich möchte mich beschweren. *I would like to* ***complain*** */* ***see the manager****.*

H 8 Der Manager hat uns eben vermieden. *The manager has just* ***seen*** */* ***avoided*** *us.*

G

Remember that **possessive adjectives** change according to gender and case.
All possessive adjective endings follow the same pattern as the indefinite article.

	nominative	**accusative**
masc	mein	mein**en**
fem	meine	meine
neut	mein	mein
plural	meine	meine

subject pronoun	**possessive adjective**
ich	mein-
du	dein-
er/sie/es/man	sein-/ihr-/sein-
wir	unser-
ihr	eu(e)r-
Sie	Ihr-
sie	ihr-

3 Circle the correct possessive adjective to complete each sentence.

1 Ich habe **meinen** / **meine** / **mein** Pass (*m*) nicht.

2 Ich brauche **meinen** / **meine** / **mein** Ruhe (*f*).

3 Leider ist das **meinen** / **meine** / **mein** Platz (*m*).

4 **Meinen** / **Meine** / **Mein** Bett (*nt*) ist kaputt.

5 **Meinen** / **Meine** / **Mein** Schlafzimmer (*nt*) ist schmutzig.

6 Er hat **meinen** / **meine** / **mein** Änderung (*f*) am Computer gemacht.

Try to work out the meaning of the sentences as you do the exercises. Don't be disheartened if you don't know the words yet! Use the glossary at the end of the module to help you.

4 Complete each sentence using a possessive adjective from the box.

Ihre   sein   ihr   euer   unsere   ihren

Check the case and gender to help you.

1 Draußen gibt es .... Stuhl (*m*). *Outside there is her chair.*

2 .... Geräusch (*nt*) war unglaublich laut. *His noise was unbelievably loud.*

3 .... Tür (*f*) war nicht sauber. *Our door was not clean.*

H 4 .... Mitarbeiter (*pl*) sind nicht freundlich. *Your (formal) employees are not friendly.*

H 5 .... Schaden (*m*) ist groß. *Your (plural, informal) damage is big.*

H 6 .... Zustand (*m*) war nicht gut. *Their condition was not good.*

H 5 Complete these sentences by translating the words in brackets into German.

1 Doch! .... (*My*) Decke (*f*) ist .... (*dirty*).

2 .... (*Their*) Einrichtung (*f*) ist sehr .... (*old*).

3 Zum Glück war .... (*our*) Zimmer (*nt*) .... (*clean*).

4 Er vergisst .... (*no one*).

5 Sie verpasst oft .... (*her flight*).

6 Wie ist .... (*your (formal) room number*)?

F 6 Translate these sentences into English.

1 Das Fenster ist kaputt. ....

2 Leider habe ich mein Laptop vergessen. ....

3 Gestern haben wir unseren Flug verpasst. ....

4 Mein Zimmer ist nicht sauber. ....

5 Ich möchte etwas sagen. ....

H 7 Translate this paragraph into German.

We want to complain because there are many problems. We have forgotten our luggage and I have lost my passport. Our room is dirty and our chairs are broken. The blanket is not clean and the lights don't work. The food is not tasty. The employees were unfriendly and no one helped us.

....

....

....

....

....

....

4 Wie waren die Schulferien?

- Using past participles with inseparable prefixes
- **H** Using prepositions with the genitive

1 Draw lines to match up the English with the German nouns.

1 island	**a** das Café
2 degree	**b** der Campingplatz
3 hotel	**c** der Grad
4 centre	**d** das Hotel
5 tent	**e** die Insel
6 café	**f** das Wetter
7 campsite	**g** das Zelt
8 weather	**h** das Zentrum

2 Match up the sentences with the pictures. Write the correct letter.

1 Hier war es kalt und es gab Wind. ....

2 Hier hat es geregnet. Es war nass und sehr kalt. ....

3 Hier war es heiß und es gab viel Sonne. Es war sehr trocken. ....

4 Hier war es kalt und neblig. Es gab keine Sonne. ....

5 Hier hat es geschneit. Es gab viel Schnee. ....

6 Hier gab es Regen und es war warm. ....

a 
b 
c 
d 
e 
f 

3 Underline the past participle in each sentence.

1 Er hat seinen Pass verloren.

2 Sie hat dort gezeltet.

3 Wir haben leckeres Essen gegessen.

4 Zuerst habe ich das lokale Museum besucht.

5 Ich bin einkaufen gegangen.

6 Ich habe das leckere Essen empfohlen.

> **G**
> Most verbs form their past participle by adding *ge-* and *-t* to the stem of the verb.
> *wohnen* → *ich habe **ge**wohn**t***
> Some verbs have inseparable prefixes (e.g. *be-*, *emp-* and *ver-*) and don't add *ge-* to the start of the verb. Some also don't change to *-t* at the end.
> *besuchen* → *ich habe **be**such**t***
> *empfehlen* → *ich habe **empf**ohl**en***
> *verlieren* → *ich habe **ver**lor**en***
> *vergessen* → *ich habe **ver**gess**en***

4 Complete these sentences with the past participle of the verb in brackets.

1 Ich bin .... (*schwimmen*)

2 Ich habe auf dem Campingplatz .... (*zelten*)

3 Ich habe das Buch .... (*empfehlen*)

4 Ich habe meine Tasche .... (*verlieren*)

5 Ich habe meinen Pass .... (*vergessen*)

6 Ich habe meine Eltern .... (*besuchen*)

H 7 Ich habe auf dem Stuhl .... (*sitzen*)

> The verb *sitzen* is irregular in the perfect tense. Look it up in the verb table on page 238 of your Student Book.

G

H Some prepositions always take the **genitive** case in German.

während during, whereas
statt instead of
trotz despite
wegen because of
außerhalb outside of
innerhalb inside of

Note that for masculine and neuter nouns, you add *-s* to the end of the noun (or *-es* if the noun has one syllable): *während **des** Jahr<u>es</u>* during the year

	masc	fem	neut	pl
nominative	der	die	das	die
genitive	des	der	des	der

H 5 Complete these sentences with the correct form of the article. Then translate the sentences into English.

1 Trotz .... Wetters haben wir eine Weile draußen gewartet.

....

2 Während .... Urlaubs flog ich nach Deutschland.

....

3 Wir haben den Bus statt .... Straßenbahn genommen.

....

4 Außerhalb .... Hotels gab es ein Schwimmbad.

....

5 Der Bus hält innerhalb .... Campingplatzes.

....

6 Wegen .... Regens habe ich einen Hut getragen.

....

F 6 Translate these sentences into German.

1 I like staying in a hotel. ....

2 I go with my family because it's great.

....

3 We don't like camping because it's not comfortable.

....

4 It was hot and there was rain. ....

5 I visited a museum. ....

H 7 Translate this paragraph into English.

Diesen Sommer bin ich mit meiner Familie nach Deutschland gefahren. Wir haben auf einem Campingplatz übernachtet. Innerhalb des Campingplatzes gab es einen See und ein Café. Ich habe jeden Tag Eis bestellt. Das Wetter war meistens gut. Es hat ein bisschen geregnet und es gab Wind, aber es war heiß.

....

....

....

5 Ich möchte um die Welt reisen!

Using interrogative and demonstrative adjectives

1 Unjumble the letters to write the German nouns correctly. Then translate the words into English.

1 sucheB ....

2 toBo ....

3 hecüK ....

4 rultKu ....

5 laM ....

6 eSe ....

7 Sdrant ....

8 blauUr ....

9 geW ....

Use the glossary to look up any words that are unfamiliar and try to learn them.

2 Complete each sentence using a verb from the box.

spazieren probieren schwimmen besuchen reisen warten mieten

1 Wir werden wieder eine Ferienwohnung ....

2 Er möchte das Essen ....

3 In der Zukunft werde ich nach Deutschland ....

4 Ihr werdet in den Seen ....

5 Ich möchte jeden Tag .... gehen.

6 Ich muss auf meine Schwester ....

7 Wenn das möglich ist, werde ich die Museen ....

3 Complete these German sentences with the correct form of the interrogative adjective (*welch-*).

1 .... Küche (*f*) ist besser? *Which cuisine is better?*

2 .... Tag (*m*) ist möglich? *What day is possible?*

3 .... See (*m*) ist ideal? *Which lake is ideal?*

4 .... Meer (*nt*) ist kalt? *Which sea is cold?*

5 .... Berg (*m*) ist hoch? *Which mountain is high?*

6 .... Dörfer (*pl*) sind schön? *Which villages are beautiful?*

G

To say 'which ...?' in the nominative case, use the **interrogative adjective *welch-*** with the correct ending to agree with the noun that follows.

masc	***Welcher*** *Weg ist schneller?* Which way is quicker?
fem	***Welche*** *Insel ist besser?* Which island is better?
neut	***Welches*** *Meer ist tiefer?* Which sea is deeper?
pl	***Welche*** *Museen sind interessanter?* Which museums are more interesting?

4 Complete these German sentences with the correct form of the demonstrative adjective (*dies-*).

1 .... Boot (*nt*) ist schnell. *This boat is fast.*

2 .... Museen (*pl*) sind interessant. *These museums are interesting.*

3 .... Seen (*pl*) sind warm. *These lakes are warm.*

4 .... Schwimmbad (*nt*) ist alt. *This swimming pool is old.*

5 .... Besuch (*m*) ist wichtig. *This visit is important.*

6 .... Sonne (*f*) ist zu heiß. *This sun is too hot.*

G

To say 'this ...' or 'these ...', use the **demonstrative adjective *dies-***, which follows the same pattern as ***welch-***.

masc ***Dieser*** *Weg ist schneller.* This way is quicker.

fem ***Diese*** *Insel ist schöner.* This island is more beautiful.

neut ***Dieses*** *Meer ist tiefer.* This sea is deeper.

pl ***Diese*** *Museen sind interessanter.* These museums are more interesting.

H 5 Complete these sentences by translating the words in brackets into German.

1 Dieser .... (*excursion*) ist interessant.

2 Am nächsten Tag werde ich dieses Schloss .... (*visit*).

3 Ich würde auf diesem Strand in der .... (*sun*) liegen.

4 .... (*Which*) Bus fährt dahin?

5 Inzwischen .... (*would like*) ich in diese Stadt fahren.

6 Das Schloss ist spannend sowie die .... (*museums*).

F 6 Translate these sentences into English.

1 Ich fahre mit dem Boot. ....

2 Dieser Tag ist sehr lang. ....

3 Wohin möchtest du fahren? ....

4 Das Wetter war nicht sehr gut. ....

5 Ich will nach Berlin fahren, weil es interessant ist. ....

....

H 7 Translate this paragraph into German.

In the holidays I will travel by plane to Germany. I would like to visit these castles and these museums. I will try the local cuisine and go to these restaurants. It will be fun. If I had time, I would go to the beach and lie in the sun.

....

....

....

....

....

Glossary

bold = this word will appear in Higher exams only

(an)bieten	*(to) offer*
Abfahrt (f)	*departure*
am besten	*(the) best (post-noun)*
am nächsten	*the next, nearest (post-noun)*
an	*on, at*
Änderung (f)	*change, alteration*
ankommen	*(to) arrive | arriving*
Ankunft (f)	*arrival*
Antwort (f)	*answer, reply*
antworten (auf)	*(to) answer, reply (to) | answering, replying (to)*
Aufmerksamkeit (f)	*attention*
Ausflug (m)	*excursion, trip, outing*
außerhalb	*outside of*
äußerst	*extremely*
Bad (nt)	*bathroom, bath, spa*
bauen	*(to) build*
beantworten	*(to) answer | answering*
beliebt	*popular*
bequem	*comfortable, comfortably*
Berg (m)	*mountain*
Berliner	*(of) Berlin*
besichtigen	*(to) view, visit*
bestimmt	*special, certainly, definitely*
Besuch (m)	*visit*
besuchen	*(to) visit, attend (school) | visiting, attending (school)*
Besucher (m)	*visitor*
Bett (nt)	*bed*
bezahlen	*(to) pay | paying*
billig	*cheap, cheaply*
bitte (schön)	*please, I beg your pardon, you're welcome*
bitten (um)	*(to) request, ask (for)*
Blick (m)	*look, view, glance*
Boot (nt)	*boat*
brauchen	*(to) need, require | needing, requiring*
Brief (m)	*letter*
Café (nt)	*café*
Campingplatz (m)	*campsite*
dahin	*there, to that place*
danke (schön)	*thank you, thanks*
danken	*(to) thank*
Decke (f)	*ceiling, blanket*
Detail (nt)	*detail*
dicht	*thick, dense*
dies- (er, e, es) (m, f, nt)	*this, that*
doch	*however, but, yes (in answer to negative question)*
Doppelzimmer (nt)	*double room, twin room*
dort	*there*
draußen	*outside*
eben	*just, now*
echt	*real, really, genuine, genuinely*
ehemalig	*former*
Eindruck (m)	*impression*
Einrichtung (f)	*furnishings*
Einzelzimmer (nt)	*single room*
empfehlen	*(to) recommend | recommending*

		😐	🙂	😎
enorm	*enormous, enormously*			
entdecken	*(to) discover*			
Erinnerung (f)	*memory*			
ermüdend	*tiring*			
Fenster (nt)	*window*			
flog	*(I, she, he, it) flew*			
Flug (m)	*flight*			
Fluss (m)	*river*			
Frau (f)	*Mrs, wife, woman*			
frei	*free, freely, available, vacant, unoccupied*			
Frühstück (nt)	*breakfast*			
funktionieren	*(to) function, work / functioning, working*			
Gebäude (nt)	*building*			
genau	*exact, exactly*			
genießen	*(to) enjoy*			
genug	*enough*			
Gepäck (nt)	*luggage*			
Geräusch (nt)	*noise*			
(aux) ... geschwommen	*swam / (have, has) swum*			
(aux) ... gesessen	*sat / (have, has) sat*			
Glück (nt)	*luck*			
Grad (m)	*degree (temperature)*			
günstig	*cheap, good*			
hält	*(she, he, it, one) stops, holds / is stopping, holding*			
halten	*(to) stop, hold / stopping, holding*			
hältst	*(you (sing informal)) stop, hold / are stopping, holding*			
heiß	*hot*			
hin	*to something, in that direction, there*			
historisch	*historical, historically*			
Hotel (nt)	*hotel*			
ideal	*ideal*			
Ihre	*your (formal) (f, pl)*			
Information (f)	*information*			
inklusive	*including*			
innerhalb	*inside of, within*			
Insel (f)	*island*			
insgesamt	*in all, altogether, in total*			
inzwischen	*in the meantime*			
Jahrhundert (nt)	*century*			
kalt	*cold*			
kaputt	*broken*			
kennenlernen	*(to) get to know / getting to know*			
klar	*clear, clearly*			
Koffer (m)	*suitcase*			
Kraft (f)	*strength, power, energy*			
Kreditkarte (f)	*credit card*			
Küche (f)	*kitchen, cuisine*			
Kultur (f)	*culture*			
Kurs (m)	*exchange rate, course*			
Küste (f)	*coast*			
landen	*(to) land / landing*			
Landschaft (f)	*countryside, scenery, landscape*			
lässt	*(you (sing informal)) let, allow, leave / are letting, allowing, leaving / (she, he, it, one) lets, allows, leaves / is letting, allowing, leaving*			
laut	*loud, loudly, noisy*			

lecker	*delicious, deliciously, tasty, tastily*
leider	*unfortunately*
liegen	*(to) lie, be lying (down), be situated*
Linie (f)	*line*
lokal	*local, locally*
Luft (f)	*air*
mag	*(I) like | am liking | (she, he, it, one) likes | is liking*
magst	*(you (sing informal)) like | are liking*
Mal (nt)	*time, occasion*
Manager (m)	*manager*
Mann (m)	*man, husband*
Meer (nt)	*sea, ocean*
mieten	*(to) hire, rent | hiring, renting*
Mitarbeiter (m)	*employee*
möglich	*possible*
Museen (pl)	*museums*
Museum (nt)	*museum*
nass	*wet*
natürlich	*of course, natural(ly)*
neblig	*foggy*
nennen; sich nennen	*(to) name, call (to) be called*
nichts	*nothing*
niemand	*no one (subj)*
niemanden	*no one (obj)*
nur	*only*
oben	*above, upstairs*
öffnen	*(to) open | opening*
Ohrhörer (pl)	*earbuds*
Ort (m)	*place, location, town*
Pass (m)	*passport*
Platz (m)	*square, seat, space, place*
praktisch	*practical, practically*
probieren; anprobieren; ausprobieren	*(to) try | trying; (to) try on | trying on; (to) try out | trying out*
Regen (m)	*rain*
Region (f)	*region*
regnen	*(to) rain | raining*
Reise (f)	*journey, trip*
reisen	*(to) travel | travelling*
reservieren	*(to) reserve, book | reserving, booking*
Reservierung (f)	*booking, reservation*
riesig	*huge, great*
Ruhe (f)	*silence, peace*
ruhig	*quiet(ly), calm(ly), peaceful(ly)*
Sand (m)	*sand*
sauber	*clean, cleanly*
Schaden (m)	*damage*
Schlafzimmer (nt)	*bedroom*
schließen	*(to) close, shut | closing, shutting*
Schloss (nt)	*castle*
schmutzig	*dirty, dirtily*
Schnee (m)	*snow*
schneien	*(to) snow | snowing*
Schwimmbad (nt)	*swimming pool*
Schwimmen (nt)	*swimming*
See (m)	*lake*
Seen (pl)	*lakes*
Sei ...!	*Be ...! (sing informal)*

seid	*(you (pl informal)) are | are being*			
Seid ...!	*Be ...! (pl informal)*			
Seien Sie ...!	*Be ...! (formal)*			
Seite (f)	*side, page*			
sich beschweren	*(to) complain*			
Sonne (f)	*sun*			
sowie	*as well as, plus*			
spazieren (gehen)	*(to) (go for a) walk, stroll | going for a walk, walking, strolling*			
Städte (pl)	*towns, cities*			
Strand (m)	*beach*			
Straße (f)	*street, road*			
Stuhl (m)	*chair*			
Telefon (nt), am Telefon	*(tele)phone, on the phone*			
teuer	*dear, expensive, expensively*			
tief	*deep, deeply*			
Tourist (m)	*tourist*			
Touristen-information (f)	*tourist information office*			
traditionell	*traditional, traditionally*			
trocken	*dry*			
Tür (f)	*door*			
übernachten	*(to) spend the night, stay*			
unglaublich	*incredible, incredibly*			
unterwegs	*on the way, en route*			
Urlaub (m)	*holiday, vacation*			
vergessen	*(to) forget | forgetting*			
vergisst	*(you (sing informal)) forget | are forgetting | (she, he, it, one) forgets | is forgetting*			
verlieren	*(to) lose | losing*			
vermeiden	*(to) avoid*			
verpassen	*(to) miss (the bus) | missing (the bus)*			
virtuell	*virtual*			
Vorschlag (m)	*suggestion, proposal*			
Wald (m)	*wood, forest*			
warm	*warm, warmly*			
warten (auf)	*(to) wait (for) | waiting (for)*			
was für?	*what kind of?*			
wechseln	*(to) change, exchange | changing, exchanging*			
Weg (m)	*way, route, road, path*			
Weile (f)	*while*			
weit	*far, widely*			
Welt (f)	*world*			
werdet	*(you (pl informal)) become | are becoming | will (aux)*			
Wetter (nt)	*weather*			
wieder	*again*			
Wind (m)	*wind*			
WLAN (nt)	*wifi*			
wohin	*where ... to?*			
würde	*(I, she, he, it) would*			
zahlreich	*numerous, many*			
Zelt (nt)	*tent*			
zelten	*(to) go camping | going camping*			
Zentrum (nt)	*centre*			
Zimmer (nt)	*room*			
zuerst	*first of all, firstly*			
Zukunft (f)	*future*			
Zustand (m)	*state, condition*			

Kulturzone Wir verbessern die Welt!

F Revising prepositions with accusative and dative

1 Read this paragraph. Translate the bold words/phrases into English on a separate sheet.

Die **Geschwister** sind in der Schweiz **geboren** und sind **danach** nach Deutschland gekommen. Sie sind **nicht binär** und haben ein **Projekt** für **Transgender-Menschen** gemacht. Sie möchten, dass alle Menschen sicher sind. Sie meinen, wir sollen alle **akzeptieren**.

G

Some prepositions are always used with either the accusative or the dative. However, **dual-case prepositions** take the **accusative** when there is **movement** involved and the **dative** when there is **no movement**.

accusative prepositions	**dative prepositions**	**dual-case prepositions** (accusative or dative)
für – *for* ohne – *without*	mit – *with* nach – *to, after* von – *from, of* aus – *out of, from*	in – *in* vor – *in front of, ago*

The **definite** and **indefinite articles** change according to the case that follows the preposition.

	masc	**fem**	**neut**	**pl**
accusative	d**en** ein**en**	die eine	das ein	die –
dative	d**em** ein**em**	d**er** ein**er**	d**em** ein**em**	den –

Remember that there are short forms of some prepositions and articles.

in das → ins

in dem → im

Movement: *Ich gehe **ins** Sportzentrum.*

No movement: *Ich bin **im** Sportzentrum.*

2 Underline the preposition in each sentence. Then circle the correct form of the article to complete each sentence.

1 Das Projekt ist in **die / der / das** Türkei (*f*).

2 Sie arbeiten gemeinsam für **eine / einem / einer** bessere Welt (*f*).

3 Sie möchten mit **das / dem / den** Projekt (*nt*) etwas verändern.

4 Er ist vor **ein / einem / einen** Jahr (*nt*) nach Deutschland gekommen.

5 Am Montag fahren sie in **die / der / das** Schweiz (*f*).

Try to work out the meaning of the sentences as you do the exercises. Use the glossary at the end of the module to help you.

3 Underline the preposition in each sentence. Then fill in the correct forms of the definite article.

1 Sie hat von .... Projekt (*nt*) in .... Schweiz (*f*) gehört.

2 Er steht mit .... Lehrerin (*f*) vor .... Schule (*f*).

3 Sie fährt mit .... Rollstuhl (*m*) in .... Supermarkt (*m*).

4 Sie kommen mit .... Essen (*nt*) aus .... Einkaufszentrum (*nt*).

5 Sie macht nach .... Prüfung (*f*) eine Party in .... Garten (*nt*).

stehen *to stand*

4 Translate these sentences into German on a separate sheet.

1 She works for a world without discrimination.

2 She was born in Turkey.

3 She has won many prizes.

4 She came to Austria a year ago.

5 She believes we should accept all people with disabilities.

H Using more prepositions with the genitive

H 1 Complete these sentences by translating the words in brackets into German.

1 Er ist .... und lebt seit beinahe 30 Jahren irgendwo in der Schweiz. (*writer*)

2 Es gibt hier viele ausländische .... und er hilft allen. (*refugees*)

3 Er hat dabei teilweise großen .... (*success*)

4 Er arbeitet für einen guten .... und hat viele gute Ergebnisse. (*purpose*)

5 Er macht deutlich große .... und tut alles, damit sie sich in der Schweiz wohlfühlen. (*progress*)

G

H Remember that some prepositions in German always take the **genitive** case:

außerhalb	*außerhalb* **des** *Landes*	outside of
innerhalb	*innerhalb* **des** *Landes*	inside of
trotz	*trotz* **des** *Fortschritts*	despite
während	*während* **der** *60er Jahre*	during
wegen	*wegen sein***er** *Arbeit*	because of

	masculine	feminine	neuter	plural
definite article	d**es**	d**er**	d**es**	d**er**
indefinite article	ein**es**	ein**er**	ein**es**	–

The genitive is also used to show possession:

der Zweck **der** *Frage*	the purpose of the question
*das Ziel sein***es** *Lebens*	the goal of his life
die Hälfte **der** *Tiere*	half of the animals

H 2 Underline the preposition, then circle the correct form of the article to complete each sentence.

1 Er hat viel gelitten und wurde wegen **seiner / seines** Arbeit kritisiert.

2 Er war für die Flüchtlinge zuständig und hat ihnen während **des / der** Ferien geholfen.

3 Außerhalb **der / des** Arbeitszeit kämpft er für die Rechte von Minderheiten.

4 Innerhalb **der / des** Stadtzentrums gibt es weder sichere Orte für Menschen mit Behinderungen noch genügend Hilfe.

5 Trotz **des / der** Fortschritts bei den Rechten für Transgender-Menschen gibt es immer noch viel Diskriminierung.

The masculine and neuter nouns are easy to spot: they have an **-s** or **-es** at the end. The others must therefore be feminine or plural.

H 3 Complete each sentence starter with the correct genitive form of the definite article. Then draw lines to match up the sentence halves.

1 Während .... Urlaubs

2 Trotz .... Kritik an seinen Büchern

3 Wegen .... Erfolgs ist er von Österreich

4 Innerhalb .... Hauses gibt es

a wurde er der beste Schriftsteller genannt.

b keine Diskriminierung.

c nach Deutschland gegangen.

d hat der Lehrer ärmeren Kindern geholfen.

H 4 Translate this paragraph into German on a separate sheet.

My role model is a writer who fights for a better society. The purpose of his life is to help all children inside and outside the country. Despite his success, he is normal and very nice. I love him because of his great books! We should all help to make the world better.

1 Was ist dir wichtig?

Using verbs followed by prepositions

1 Translate these German cognates and near-cognates into English.

1 das Internet ....

2 der Artikel ....

3 der Start ....

4 die Aktion ....

5 die Diskussion ....

6 der Aspekt ....

H 7 der Experte ....

Cognates are words that look similar, and have the same meaning, in both English and German.

2 Complete each sentence using words from the box.

Sorgen Bildung
Lösung Freiheit
Sicherheit Themen

1 Welche .... sind allgemein für dich und deine Generation wichtig?

2 Für mich ist meine .... und deswegen die Schule sehr wichtig.

3 Mir ist meine .... wichtig; ich will mich überall frei bewegen.

H 4 Alle Menschen sollen sich sicher fühlen, also ist für mich .... für alle Menschen das Wichtigste.

H 5 Wir machen uns große .... um den Rassismus in unserem Land und ich hoffe mit meinen Freunden, dass es bald eine .... dafür gibt.

Use the glossary to look up any words that are unfamiliar, and try to learn them.

G

Many verbs in German are followed by a **preposition**. Note which case each preposition takes after a verb and make the article agree with the gender of the noun.

sich interessieren ***für*** (+ acc)	to be interested **in**	*hoffen* ***auf*** (+ acc)	to hope **for**
sich freuen ***auf*** (+ acc)	to look forward **to**	*warten* ***auf*** (+ acc)	to wait **for**

To refer to something you have already mentioned, add ***da-*** to the preposition:

Ich interessiere mich ***dafür***. I am interested **in it**.

If the preposition begins with a vowel, add ***dar-***.

Ich freue mich ***darauf***. I am looking forward **to it**.

You also need this form of the preposition if a clause with *dass* follows the verb, as in exercise 3.

H Other examples of prepositions:

hinter – ***dahinter*** behind it; *neben* – ***daneben*** next to it

unter – ***darunter*** underneath it; *zwischen* – ***dazwischen*** in between them

H When asking questions, add ***wo(r)-*** to the preposition:

Wovor *hast du Angst?* **What** are you afraid **of**?

Worauf *wartest du?* **What** are you waiting **for**?

3 Circle the correct word to complete each sentence.

1 Ich freue mich **dafür / darauf**, dass ich nächste Woche Ferien habe.

2 Ich hoffe **dafür / darauf**, dass alle Menschen dieselben Freiheiten haben.

H 3 Ich warte **dafür / darauf**, dass ich endlich studieren kann.

H 4 Ich interessiere mich **dafür / darauf**, was in der Welt passiert.

4 Underline the preposition in each question. Then complete each answer using a word from the box.

davon	daraus
damit	darin
davor	darüber
darauf	

1 Hoffst du auf eine gute Zukunft? *Ja, ich hoffe ....*

2 Bist du mit deiner Vergangenheit zufrieden? *Ja, ich bin .... zufrieden.*

3 Hast du von diesem Artikel gehört? *Ja, ich habe .... gehört.*

H 4 Hast du Angst vor Diskussionen? *Ja, ich habe Angst ....*

H 5 Habt ihr über Cyberkriminalität gesprochen? *Ja, wir haben .... gesprochen.*

H 6 Was kann man aus diesem Artikel lernen? *Man kann .... lernen, Umweltprobleme zu lösen.*

H 7 Was ist der Sinn in dieser Aktion? *Ich sehe den Sinn dieser Aktion ...., dass Experten mit Menschen über Probleme sprechen und nicht schweigen.*

H 5 Draw lines to match up the questions with the answers.

1 Woran denkst du?
2 Wovon hast du gehört?
3 Womit bist du zufrieden?
4 Wozu braucht ihr das Internet?
5 Worüber habt ihr diskutiert?
6 Wofür kämpft ihr?
7 Was ist das Gute an der Diskussion?

a Wir brauchen das Internet dazu, um uns über die aktuelle Situation zu informieren.
b Ich denke daran, dass ich heute irgendwann noch meine Hausaufgaben machen muss.
c Wir haben darüber diskutiert, wie man irgendetwas für die Umwelt tun kann.
d Das Gute daran ist, dass wir über das Thema gesprochen haben.
e Wir kämpfen dafür, dass sich alle Menschen sicher fühlen können.
f Ich habe davon gehört, dass viele Menschen auf der Welt an Hunger leiden.
g Ich bin damit zufrieden, dass ich ein gutes Leben habe.

F 6 Translate these sentences into German.

1 My freedom is very important to me. ....

2 He is interested in the environment. ....

3 I hope for a good future for me and my friends.

....

4 I am very interested in it. ....

5 I will study maths at university and I'm looking forward to it.

....

H 7 Translate this paragraph into English on a separate sheet.

Das größte Problem in unserer Gesellschaft ist der Rassismus. Die Expertin kämpft dafür, dass es keine Diskriminierung gibt. Auch die Sicherheit ist ein wichtiger Aspekt. Aber das Wichtigste ist, dass alle Menschen die gleichen Rechte haben sollen. Ich mache mir große Sorgen um die Zukunft und möchte nicht schweigen, sondern darüber sprechen.

H Adjectives can be used to create neuter nouns by adding a capital letter and **-e**.
gut: ***Das Gute** ist* ... The good thing is ...
Superlative forms can also be used by adding **-ste**.
schlimm: ***Das Schlimmste** daran ist* ... The worst thing about it is ...

2 Unser armer Planet
Revising compound nouns

1 Unjumble the letters to rewrite the nouns correctly. Add the definite article (*der*, *die* or *das*) and translate them into English.

1 laGs ....
2 aBmu ....
3 Ghrefa ....
4 ltUemw ....
5 tempuTerar ....
H 6 lmKia ....
H 7 ülMl ....

2 Complete each sentence using a verb from the box.

ausmachen kaufen sammeln fahren brauchen
trennen wegwerfen schützen verbieten

1 Wir müssen die armen Tiere, die in Gefahr sind, retten und ....
2 Wenn wir aus dem Zimmer gehen, sollen wir das Licht ....
3 Wenige Deutsche .... elektrische Autos.
4 Alle Menschen .... reine Luft und sauberes Wasser.
5 Man soll Plastik .... und nicht ...., oder total ....
H 6 Wir sollen nachhaltige Produkte ....
H 7 Man muss den Müll ....

3 Complete each compound noun using a word part from the box.

1 die Web..................
2 das Trink..................
3 das Umwelt..................
4 die Klein..................
H 5 das Gegen..................
H 6 das Baum..................

wasser
problem
seite
blatt
stadt
teil

G
Remember that **compound nouns** can be formed from:
- two nouns:
Musik + Instrument → das Musikinstrument
- a verb stem and a noun:
laufen + Schuhe → die Laufschuhe
- an adjective and a noun:
groß + Stadt → die Großstadt

When the first noun ends in a consonant, it is common to add an **s** to link the words:
*Einkauf + Zentrum → das Einkauf**s**zentrum*
The gender of a compound noun will always be determined by the gender of the final noun in the word.

4 Write the correct definite article (*der*, *die* or *das*) for each compound noun. Then translate the nouns into English.

1 .... Verkehrsmittel ....
2 .... Glasflasche ....
3 .... Gesundheitssystem ....
H 4 .... Klimawandel ....
H 5 .... Umweltverschmutzung ....

H 5 Underline the compound noun in each sentence. Then translate the noun into English.

1 Ich habe bewusst angefangen, Plastikflaschen zu sammeln und nicht wegzuwerfen.

....

2 Ich möchte mich mehr über den Klimaschutz und erneuerbare Energien informieren.

....

3 Fast jeden Augenblick droht den Flüchtlingen Gefahr.

....

4 Ein sehr schlimmes Problem ist der Verlust von vielen Tierarten.

....

5 Experten sollen Instrumente gegen die Luftverschmutzung entwickeln.

....

Some words may be new to you. Use a dictionary or the glossary to find their meaning. A synonym for one of the words is *der Moment*.

F 6 Translate these sentences into English.

1 Plastikflaschen sind ein großes Umweltproblem.

....

....

2 Auf der Webseite kann man sich informieren.

....

3 Alle Länder sollen ein gutes Gesundheitssystem haben.

....

4 Die Umweltstudie sagt, dass viele Tiere in Gefahr sind.

....

5 Viele Länder haben kein reines Trinkwasser und das ist gefährlich.

....

Look out for cognates and near-cognates (words that are the same or similar in both languages), and similarities between nouns and adjectives.

H 7 Translate this paragraph into German.

In my opinion, the worst problem is air pollution. I think everyone should drive electric cars and use renewable energy. It's also very important to buy sustainable products. We must also consciously separate and recycle our rubbish. Have you already started to save the climate?

....

....

....

....

....

....

3 Wir können alle etwas machen!

Using *wollen* (to want to) • Using verbs in three time frames

1 Circle the odd one out.

1 verlassen / umweltfreundlich / sammeln / recyceln

2 Papier / elektrisch / Strom / Plastik

3 manchmal / immer / retten / ab und zu

4 anrufen / wegwerfen / ausmachen / kaufen

H 5 teilnehmen / nutzen / verantwortlich / trennen

2 Underline the verb(s) in each sentence. Write down the infinitive(s) and translate it/them into English.

1 Wir sparen jeden Tag Strom und Wasser. ....

2 Ich sammle ab und zu leere Plastikflaschen. ....

3 Er recycelt oft Papier, denn Recycling ist wichtig! ....

4 Ich mache immer das Licht aus. ....

H 5 Fängst du an, Müll zu trennen?

....

H 6 Du musst aufhören, immer so viel neue Kleidung zu kaufen.

....

Some sentences may have more than one verb. Use a dictionary or the glossary to find any that you don't know. Tip: one separable verb is a synonym for *beginnen*, and another for *beenden*.

G

Use ***wollen*** + infinitive to express what people want to do.

ich will	wir wollen
du willst	ihr wollt
er/sie/es/man will	Sie/sie wollen

When using **modal verbs**, remember that the second verb (the infinitive) must go to the end of the sentence.

*Wir **wollen** die Umwelt schützen.*

We **want to** protect the environment.

Don't confuse *wollen* (want to) with *werden* (will). To express the future, use *werden* + infinitive.

*Wir **werden** die Umwelt schützen.*

We **will** protect the environment.

H The modal verb ***wollen*** can also be used with a noun on its own:

*Wir **wollen** den Sieg über den Rassismus.*

We **want** the victory over racism.

3 Complete these German translations.

1 I want to save electricity more often. *Ich* .... *öfter Strom* ....

2 Do you want to buy fewer new clothes? .... *ihr weniger neue Kleidung* ....?

3 We want to recycle more paper and plastic. *Wir* .... *mehr Papier und Plastik* ....

4 Mrs Schmidt, do you want to always switch off the light when you leave the room?

Frau Schmidt, ... *Sie immer das Licht* ...., *wenn sie das Zimmer* ....?

5 Mark, do you want to go to school on foot or go by car? *Mark,* .... *du zu Fuß zur Schule* .... *oder mit dem Auto* ....?

H 6 People don't want tins but rather glass bottles. *Die Menschen* .... *keine Dosen, sondern lieber Glasflaschen.*

4 Complete these sentences with the correct form of the verb in brackets in German.

1 Ich werde jeden Tag Plastik .... (*recycle*)

2 Sie wollen jetzt öfter mit dem Fahrrad zur Schule .... (*drive, go*)

3 Hast du schon wieder neue Kleidung ....? (*buy*)

4 .... du Plastikflaschen? (*collect*)

5 Ich werde nie wieder Papier .... (*throw away*)

6 Marie hat normalerweise immer das Licht ...., wenn sie die Küche verlassen hat. (*switch off*)

Watch out for separable verbs.

G

Understanding and using three time frames in your work will help you to target higher grades.

Present: *Ich **kaufe** umweltfreundliche Produkte.*

Past: *Ich **habe** umweltfreundliche Produkte **gekauft**.*

Future: *Ich **werde** umweltfreundliche Produkte **kaufen**.*

Remember where the prefix goes on separable verbs in the present tense. Also remember where **-ge-** goes in the perfect tense.

Present: *Ich **rufe** meine Mutter **an**.*

Past: *Ich **habe** meine Mutter **angerufen**.*

Future: *Ich **werde** meine Mutter **anrufen**.*

H 5 Underline the verb(s) in each sentence and write down the tense each sentence is in. Then rewrite the sentence in the tense indicated in brackets.

1 Ich war Mitglied in einem Verein für Klimaschutz. ....
(*future*) ....

2 Wir sind alle für die Umwelt verantwortlich. ....
(*future*) ....

3 Ich kaufe immer nachhaltige Produkte, aber das genügt nicht. ....
(*perfect*) ....

4 Wir tragen heute alle die Verantwortung für unsere Zukunft. ....
(*perfect*) ....

5 Wir werden an Diskussionen zum Thema Umweltschutz teilnehmen. ....
(*present*) ....

F 6 Translate these sentences into German on a separate sheet.

1 I'm usually very environmentally friendly.

2 He always switches off the light.

3 She will go by bike more often.

4 We collected paper and plastic every day.

5 You want to do more for the environment in the future.

H 7 Translate this paragraph into English on a separate sheet.

Willst du keine Umweltverschmutzung und eine bessere Welt? Willst du für die Umwelt verantwortlich sein und gegen den Klimawandel kämpfen? Dann kannst du Mitglied in einem Verein werden! Dort kannst du an verschiedenen Veranstaltungen teilnehmen und in der Gesellschaft aktiv sein. Du kannst auch Geld sammeln, Projekte organisieren und dadurch der Umwelt helfen.

4 Wir wollen eine bessere Welt!

Using *man* • H Using the conditional of *sollen*

1 Draw lines to match up the German words with their English translations.

1 die Grenze	**a** truth
2 die Union	**b** citizen
3 die Erde	**c** border
4 der Sprecher	**d** star
5 die Wahrheit	**e** speaker
H **6** der Bürger	**f** Earth
H **7** der Stern	**g** union

2 Complete each sentence using a word from the box.

zahlen leben
Europäische dürfen
praktisch reisen
international

1 Die .... Union (EU) ist sehr .... und hat 27 Länder.

2 Die Menschen können oft ohne Pass ....

3 Sie können normalerweise auch mit dem Euro ...., was sehr .... ist.

4 Sie .... auch in anderen Ländern .... und arbeiten.

G

Man can be translated as 'you', 'they', 'people', 'organisations' or occasionally 'one'.
Remember when using **modal verbs** that the second verb in the sentence will be in the <u>infinitive</u> and it will be at the end of the clause.
Man ***kann*** *Geld <u>sammeln</u>.*
Man ***will*** *Kindern <u>helfen</u>.*
Man ***soll*** *Tiere <u>respektieren</u>.*
Man ***muss*** *die Situation für alle <u>verbessern</u>.*
Man ***darf*** *in die Schule <u>gehen</u>.*
H *Man* + verb can also be used to avoid the passive voice in German.
Man respektiert die Umwelt.
The environment is respected.

G

H ***Sollte-*** is the conditional form of *sollen* and means 'should'. Just as in the present tense, the conditional form of modal verbs also sends the second verb (<u>the infinitive</u>) to the end of the clause.
Man ***sollte*** *Menschenrechte <u>respektieren</u>.*
You/They/One **should** <u>respect</u> human rights.

*ich soll**te***	*wir soll**ten***
*du soll**test***	*ihr soll**tet***
*er/sie/es/man soll**te***	*Sie/sie soll**ten***

3 Rewrite each sentence, putting the words into the correct order.

1 Tiere die Man retten will ....

2 das darf trinken Wasser Man ....

3 Schule Man zu kann Fuß zur gehen ....

4 Plastik und Man sammeln recyceln soll ....

5 die Man respektieren Menschenrechte muss ....

4 Rewrite these sentences using *man*.

1 Viele Menschen können in der EU wählen. ....

2 „Ärzte ohne Grenzen" wollen kranken Menschen helfen.

....

3 Die EU-Sprecher müssen die Wahrheit sagen und die Umwelt retten.

....

4 In der Europäischen Union dürfen die Menschen oft ohne Pass reisen.

....

H 5 Globale Vereine sollten alle Kinder auf der Erde schützen.

....

H 5 Circle the correct form of the verb to complete each sentence.

1 Die EU **sollte** / **sollten** / **solltest** den Streit zwischen Ländern beenden.

2 Sie **solltest** / **sollten** / **solltet** anfangen, die weltweite Krise zu kontrollieren.

3 Man **sollte** / **solltet** / **sollten** gewiss nicht erst jetzt beginnen, den Klimawandel zu stoppen.

4 Die Menschen **sollte** / **solltet** / **sollten** mehr tun, damit Tiere in Gefahr überleben.

5 Der Klimawandel **sollten** / **solltest** / **sollte** Gegenstand der Diskussion sein.

F 6 Translate these sentences into English.

1 Du hilfst der lokalen Natur. ....

2 Man kann Tiere in Gefahr retten. ....

3 Man soll alle Religionen respektieren. ....

4 Man darf in der EU fast überall ohne Pass reisen.

....

5 „Ärzte ohne Grenzen" arbeiten global und helfen kranken Menschen.

....

H 7 Translate this paragraph into German.

The European Union has only existed since 1993. Within the EU there are 27 countries and 24 languages. Citizens who are living in an EU member state can normally travel within the EU borders without a passport. You can also pay with the euro in many EU member states. You should travel to the EU!

....

....

....

....

....

....

5 Dialog ist wichtig!

Using phrases of debating

1 Draw lines to match up the English words with their German translations.

1 risk	**a** das Wort
2 network	**b** das Netzwerk
3 vegan	**c** der Vegetarier / die Vegetarierin
4 vegetarian	**d** das Fleisch
5 alternative	**e** die Alternative
6 communication	**f** der Veganer / die Veganerin
7 word	**g** die Kommunikation
8 meat	**h** das Risiko

2 Complete each sentence using a verb from the box.

sieht ist muss
essen scheint
wirft abnehmen

1 Wenn es regnet und die Sonne nicht ...., funktioniert die Sache nicht.

2 Du solltest Vegetarier sein und kein Fleisch ....

3 Wenn man hinausgeht, ... man, dass die Windenergie funktioniert.

4 Sie .... nie Essen weg, sie isst es am nächsten Tag.

H **5** Ich .... dich warnen: Das hat eine schlimme Wirkung auf die Umwelt und zerstört sie.

H **6** Luftverschmutzung .... eine Ursache für den Klimawandel.

H **7** Mit elektrischen Autos werden die Risiken ....

When **debating in speaking** you can use certain phrases.

Das stimmt! *That is correct!*

Du hast Recht ... *You are right ...*

Meiner Meinung nach ... *In my opinion ...*

Ich meine, dass ... *I think/believe/say that ...*

Ich denke/glaube/finde, dass ... *I think/believe/find that ...*

H Ich bin der Meinung, dass ... *I'm of the opinion that ...*

H einerseits ... andererseits ... *on the one hand ... on the other hand ...*

H Im Gegenteil, ... *on the other hand ...*

H Ich behaupte (trotzdem) ... *I maintain/claim (nevertheless) ...*

H Ich bin (übrigens) davon überzeugt, dass ... *I am (by the way) convinced, that ...*

3 Separate out the words and write out the sentences on a separate sheet.

1 Dasstimmt,WindenergieisteinesaubereAlternative.

2 DuhastRecht,aberneueNetzwerkekostenvielGeld.

3 Ichfinde,dassnurGemüseessenlangweiligist.

4 Ichdenke,dassesinmeinemLandvieleUmweltproblemegibt.

5 MeinerMeinungnachistesnichtgutfürdieGesundheitwennmanzuvielFleischisst.

4 Rewrite the underlined part of each sentence, putting the words into the correct order.

1 Du hast Recht, ... ich werde versuchen das ....

2 Ich glaube, dass ... Gefühle Tiere auch haben ....

3 Meiner Meinung nach ist Fleisch lecker, aber ... gesünder Gemüse ist ....

4 Das stimmt, aber ... Vegetarier gibt wenige oft Alternativen für es

....

H 5 Das ist einerseits wahr, aber andererseits ... Gemüse mir nicht schmeckt

....

H 5 Read the sentences and translate the underlined German verbs into English using words from the box.

contributes	are lacking
prevent	cause

1 Ich bin davon überzeugt, dass Luft- und Wasserverschmutzung den Klimawandel verursachen.

....

2 Ich behaupte, dass in den Restaurants Alternativen für Vegetarier und Veganer fehlen.

....

3 Ich bin der Meinung, dass man den Klimawandel auf diese Weise verhindern kann.

....

4 Ich glaube fest daran, dass die Wasserverschmutzung zum Klimawandel beiträgt.

....

F 6 Translate these sentences into German.

1 We must protect nature. ....

2 Too much meat is not good for the environment. ....

3 I believe that solar energy works. ....

4 In my opinion, vegetarians live more healthily. ....

....

5 Yes, you're right, but there are also many alternatives. ....

....

H 7 Translate this paragraph into English.

Einerseits ist es wahr, dass die Umwelt sehr wichtig ist und dass man Tiere schützen muss. Andererseits schmeckt mir Fleisch einfach zu sehr. Ich finde, nur Gemüse essen ist langweilig. Aber vielleicht werde ich versuchen, weniger Fleisch und mehr Gemüse zu essen. Ich bin davon überzeugt, ich kann das schaffen!

....

....

....

....

....

....

Glossary

bold = this word will appear in Higher exams only

		😐	🙂	😎
abnehmen	*(to) decrease, reduce / decreasing, reducing*			
Aktion (f)	*campaign, action*			
aktuell	*current, currently*			
akzeptieren	*(to) accept / accepting*			
allgemein	*general, generally*			
Alternative (f)	*alternative*			
andererseits	*on the other hand*			
anfangen	*(to) start / starting*			
(aux) … angefangen	*started / (have, has) started*			
Angst (f)	*fear*			
arm	*poor, poorly*			
ärmer	*poorer*			
Art (f)	*type, kind, species*			
Artikel (m)	*article*			
Aspekt (m)	*aspect*			
auf diese Weise	*in this way*			
aufhören	*(to) stop / stopping*			
Augenblick (m)	*moment*			
ausländisch	*foreign*			
ausmachen	*(to) put out, switch off / putting out, switching off*			
Baum (m)	*tree*			
beenden	*(to) end / ending*			
behaupten	*(to) maintain, claim / maintaining, claiming*			
beinahe	*almost, nearly*			
beitragen zu	*(to) contribute to / contributing to*			
bewusst	*conscious, aware*			
Bildung (f)	*education*			
Blatt (nt)	*sheet, leaf*			
Bürger (m)	*citizen*			
dabei	*with it, there*			
dadurch	*through it, as a result, as a consequence*			
dahinter	*behind it*			
damit	*so that*			
damit	*with it*			
danach	*after it, afterwards*			
daneben	*next to it, beside it*			
daran, dran	*on it, at it, in the process of it*			
darauf, drauf	*on it, **onto it, at it,** to it*			
daraus	*out of it, from it*			
darin, drin, drinnen	*in it, in there, inside*			
darüber, drüber	*above it, about it*			
darunter	*under it, underneath*			
das Gute (nt)	*the good (thing)*			
davon	*from it, about it*			
davor	*before (it), in front of it*			
dazwischen	*in between, between (them), among (them)*			
der / die / das größte …	*(the) biggest …*			
derselbe, dieselbe, dasselbe	*the same*			
deswegen	*therefore, that's why*			
deutlich	*clear, clearly*			
(der) Deutsche, (ein) Deutscher (m), (die, eine) Deutsche (f), Deutsche, (die) Deutschen (pl)	*German, (the) Germans*			

Diskussion (f)	*discussion*
diskutieren (über)	*(to) discuss / discussing*
Dose (f)	*tin, can*
drohen	*(to) threaten / threatening*
einerseits	*on the one hand*
elektrisch	*electric, electrically*
entwickeln	*(to) develop / developing*
Erde (f)	*Earth*
Erfolg (m)	*success*
Ergebnis (nt)	*result*
erneuerbar	*renewable*
erst	*only, not until*
EU (f)	*European Union, EU*
europäisch	*European*
existieren	*(to) exist / existing*
Experte (m)	*expert*
Expertin (f)	*expert*
fängst ... an	*(you (sing informal)) start / are starting*
fehlen	*(to) lack, be absent, miss / lacking, being absent, missing*
Fleisch (nt)	*meat*
Flüchtling (m)	*refugee*
Fortschritt (m)	*progress*
Freiheit (f)	*freedom*
geboren	*born*
Gefahr (f)	*danger, risk*
gefährlich	*dangerous, dangerously*
Gefühl (nt)	*feeling*
Gegenstand (m)	*object*
Gegenteil (nt); im Gegenteil	*opposite; on the other hand*
(aux) ... gelitten	*suffered / (have, has) suffered*
gemeinsam	*common, mutual*
(aux) ... genannt	*named / (have, has) named*
Generation (f)	*generation*
genügen	*(to) be enough/ sufficient / being enough/ sufficient*
Geschwister (pl)	*brothers and sisters, siblings*
gewiss	*certain, certainly*
gibst	*(you (sing informal)) give / are giving*
gibt	*(she, he, it, one) gives / is giving*
Glas (nt)	*jar, glass*
global	*global, globally*
Grenze (f)	*border, frontier*
Hälfte (f)	*half*
heute	*today, nowadays*
hilfst	*(you (sing informal)) help / are helping*
hinaus	*out, beyond*
informieren	*(to) inform / informing*
international	*international, internationally*
Internet (nt)	*internet*
irgendetwas, irgendwas	*something, anything*
irgendwann	*sometime, some day*
irgendwo	*somewhere*
Klima (nt)	*climate*
Klimawandel (m)	*climate change*
Kommunikation (f)	*communication*
kontrollieren	*(to) check, control / checking, controlling*
Krise (f)	*crisis*
kritisieren	*(to) criticise / criticising*
leer	*empty*

leiden	*(to) suffer | suffering*			
Licht (nt)	*light*			
Lösung (f)	*solution*			
meinen	*(to) think, have an opinion | thinking, having an opinion*			
Mitglied (nt)	*member*			
Müll (m)	*waste, rubbish*			
nachhaltig	*sustainable, sustainably*			
Netzwerk (nt)	*network*			
nicht binär	*non-binary*			
nutzen	*(to) use | using*			
Papier (nt)	*paper*			
Plastik (nt)	*plastic*			
Produkt (nt)	*product*			
Projekt (nt)	*plan, project*			
recyceln	*(to) recycle | recycling*			
Recycling (nt)	*recycling*			
regnet	*(it) rains | (it) is raining*			
rein	*pure, clean, clear*			
retten	*(to) save (e.g. the world) | saving (e.g. the world)*			
Risiken (pl)	*risks*			
Risiko (nt)	*risk*			
Sache (f)	*thing, issue*			
sammeln	*(to) collect | collecting*			
scheinen	*(to) shine, seem, appear | shining, seeming, appearing*			
schlimm	*bad, serious*			
schmecken	*(to) taste | tasting*			
Schriftsteller (m)	*writer*			
schützen	*(to) protect | protecting*			
schweigen	*(to) be silent | being silent*			
Sicherheit (f)	*security, safety*			
Sieg (m)	*victory*			
sollte	*(I/she, he, it, one) was supposed to | should (conditional)*			
solltest	*(you (sing informal)) were supposed to | should (conditional)*			
Sorge (f)	*worry*			
Sprecher (m)	*speaker*			
Stern (m)	*star*			
stimmen	*(to) be correct | being correct*			
Streit (m)	*argument, fight*			
Strom (m)	*electricity, stream, current, river*			
Studie (f)	*study*			
teilnehmen an	*(to) take part in, participate in | taking part in, participating in*			
teilweise	*partly*			
Temperatur (f)	*temperature*			
Thema (nt)	*theme, topic, subject*			
Themen (nt)	*themes, topics, subjects*			
Tier (nt)	*animal*			
Transgender-	*transgender*			
trennen	*(to) separate | separating*			
trotzdem	*nevertheless*			
überleben	*(to) survive | surviving*			
überzeugen	*(to) convince | convincing*			
übrigens	*by the way, what's more*			
Umwelt (f)	*environment*			
umweltfreundlich	*eco-friendly*			

Union (f)	*union*
Ursache (f)	*cause*
Veganer(in) (m/f)	*vegan*
Vegetarier(in) (m/f)	*vegetarian*
verändern	*(to) change / changing*
verantwortlich	*responsible, responsibly*
Verantwortung (f)	*responsibility*
verbieten	*(to) forbid / forbidding*
Vergangenheit (f)	*past*
verhindern	*(to) prevent, hinder / preventing, hindering*
Verkehrsmittel (nt)	*means of transport*
verlassen	*(to) leave / leaving*
Verlust (m)	*loss*
Verschmutzung (f)	*pollution*
versuchen	*(to) try / trying*
verursachen	*(to) cause / causing*
wählen	*(to) choose, vote / choosing, voting*
wahr	*true*
während	*during, while, whereas*
Wahrheit (f)	*truth*
warnen	*(to) warn / warning*
Webseite (f)	*website*
weder	*neither*
weg	*away, vanished*
wegen	*because of, due to*
Weise (f)	*way, manner*
weltweit	*worldwide*
wenige	*few*
werfen	*(to) throw / throwing*
wirft	*(she, he, it, one) throws / is throwing*
Wirkung (f)	*effect*
wofür	*for what*
womit	*with which*
woran	*on what, at what*
worauf	*on what, to what*
Wort (nt)	*word*
worüber	*what about*
wovon	*from what, about what*
wovor	*what ... of, what ... in front of*
wozu	*on what, onto what, at what, to what*
zerstören	*(to) destroy / destroying*
zufrieden	*content, pleased*
zuständig	*responsible*
Zweck (m)	*purpose*

F Using *möchten* und *wollen*

1 Complete the text using the nouns in the box.

Arbeitsalltag Vorstellungen Prozent Erfahrungen Prüfungen

Wie wird meine Zukunft nach den **1** .... aussehen? Ich weiß noch nicht hundert **2** ...., aber ich habe so einige **3** .... Meine Eltern wollen, dass ich ein Medizinstudium mache. Aber ich habe mir gedacht, das ist unmöglich. Ich möchte erst berufliche **4** .... sammeln. Wie sieht ein **5** .... aus? Das will ich herausfinden und selbst sehen.

Start by looking up in the glossary any unfamiliar words in the box. The nouns ending in *-en* are plurals. *Arbeitsalltag* is a compound noun so you may need to look up one or both parts.

sieht ... aus is a conjugated form of the verb *aussehen*.

G

Use the following when you want to say what you **would like to do** or **want to do**:
Ich möchte + infinitive (= I would like to ...)
Ich will + infinitive (= I want to ..., and **not** 'I will'!)

möchten (*would like to*)	**wollen** (*want to*)
ich möchte	ich will
du möchtest	du willst
er/sie/es/man möchte	er/sie/es/man will
wir möchten	wir wollen
ihr möchtet	ihr wollt
Sie möchten	Sie wollen
sie möchten	sie wollen

Try to work out the meaning of the sentences as you do the exercises. Use the glossary at the end of the module to help you.

2 Complete each sentence using a modal verb from the box.

1 Silvia und Malik, was .... ihr nach den Prüfungen machen?
2 Herr Schiller, ... Sie weiter der Umwelt helfen?
3 Katharina, ... du im Krankenhaus arbeiten?
4 Was .... Maria nach der Schule machen?

möchten
will
möchtest
wollt

3 Complete these sentences by translating the words in brackets into German.

1 Ich .... mit älteren Menschen arbeiten, genauso wie meine Schwester. (*want*)
2 Robin .... mit Personen arbeiten, die in Gefahr sind und Hilfe brauchen. (*would like*)
3 .... ihr erst einen Beruf ausprobieren und danach vielleicht studieren? (*would like*)
4 .... du einen Job haben und 1 200 Euro im Monat verdienen? (*want*)
5 Ich .... nicht sitzen bleiben, deshalb lerne ich viel. (*would like*)

4 Translate these sentences into German on a separate sheet.

1 Should I do training?
2 I want to learn practical things.
3 After school we want to have an interesting job.
4 My friend would like to work with older people.
5 Would you like to try out a working day?

Kulturzone Ich will helfen

H Revising verbs and constructions with *zu*

H 1 Complete these sentences by translating the words in brackets into German.

1 Was man nach den Prüfungen machen will, ist eine schwierige .... (*decision*)

2 Wenn ich mit der Schule .... bin, will ich nicht gleich auf die Universität gehen. (*finished*)

3 Ich möchte etwas Gutes tun und .... praktische Dinge lernen. (*at the same time*)

4 Man hat die ...., wertvolle Kenntnisse und Erfahrungen zu sammeln. (*opportunity*)

> **G**
>
> H Remember that you need to use ***zu*** with an <u>infinitive</u> after some verbs:
>
> *hoffen* to hope
> *planen* to plan
> *(sich) entscheiden* to decide
> ***vor****schlagen* to suggest
> ***vor****haben* to intend
>
> ***Ich hoffe****, in der Zukunft auf die Uni* ***zu*** *<u>gehen</u>.*
> ***Ich habe vor****, ein soziales Jahr* ***zu*** *<u>machen</u>.*
>
> Other constructions follow the same pattern:
> *es ist (nicht) leicht, ... zu ...* it is (not) easy to ...
> *bereit sein, ... zu ...* be ready/prepared to ...
> *die Gelegenheit haben, ... zu ...* have the opportunity to ...
> *Lust haben, ... zu ...* to feel like doing something
> *statt ... zu ...* instead of ...
>
> ***Es ist nicht leicht****, eine gute Arbeit* ***zu*** *<u>finden</u>.*
> ***Ich habe Lust****, neue Länder kennen****zu****<u>lernen</u>.*
> ***Statt*** *mir einen Job* ***zu*** *<u>suchen</u>, ...*
>
> Remember that **modal verbs** in German do **not use *zu*** before the infinitive.

H 2 Rewrite these sentences using *zu* + infinitive.

> Do you remember where *zu* goes in separable verbs?

1 Ich will einen Beitrag für die Gesellschaft leisten.

Ich habe vor, ...

2 Ich möchte alte und kranke Menschen pflegen.

Ich habe entschieden, ...

3 Ich möchte auf jeden Fall verschiedene Sachen ausprobieren.

Ich habe Lust, ...

4 Ich möchte nicht sofort auf die Universität gehen, sondern erst einmal ein sogenanntes soziales Jahr machen.

Statt sofort auf die Universität ....

....

H 3 On a separate sheet, rewrite each pair of sentences as one sentence using *zu* + infinitive.

1 Ich hoffe. Ich studiere später Medizin. <u>Ich hoffe, später Medizin zu studieren.</u>

2 Außerdem bin ich bereit. Ich lerne neue Dinge.

3 Man hat die Gelegenheit. Man hilft anderen Menschen.

4 Ich finde es nicht leicht. Ich lerne neue Leute kennen.

H 4 Translate this paragraph into German on a separate sheet.

I have decided to do a social year after school. I would like to make a contribution to society and care for sick children. In this way I can work with children and at the same time learn new things. I hope to gain lots of different experiences. I plan to work in a hospital.

> Translate 'gain' with the verb meaning '(to) collect'.

1 Was wirst du nach deinen Prüfungen machen?

Using reflexive verbs

1 Unjumble the letters to rewrite the words correctly. Then translate them into English.

1 mFair ....

2 lGde ....

3 prGäesch ....

4 taKkton ....

5 rLeerh ....

H 6 esObufter ....

Noten	unbedingt
sicher	Ausbildung

2 Complete each sentence using a word from the box.

1 Ich bin mir noch nicht ...., ob ich nach der Schule an der Universität studiere.

2 Ich hoffe, dass ich eine gute .... finde, ohne zu viel Arbeit!

H 3 Ich hoffe auf gute ...., damit ich in großen Firmen Arbeit suchen kann.

H 4 Ich werde mir eine Stelle suchen, denn mein Geld ist knapp und ich will .... viel verdienen.

3 Circle the correct reflexive pronoun to complete each sentence.

1 Er setzt **sich** / **euch** / **uns** an den Tisch.

2 Ich freue **sich** / **mich** / **dich** auf meine Ferien.

3 Wir verstehen **sich** / **uns** / **euch** sehr gut mit unseren Eltern.

4 Du musst **sich** / **dich** / **euch** konzentrieren, sonst bestehst du die Prüfung nicht.

5 Elias und Layla, es ist kalt, zieht **mich** / **uns** / **euch** warm an.

H 6 Einige interessante Möglichkeiten präsentieren **mich** / **dich** / **sich** bei meiner Jobsuche.

G

Reflexive verbs are used with a pronoun which usually goes straight after the verb.

ich interessiere ***mich***	*wir interessieren* ***uns***
du interessierst ***dich***	*ihr interessiert* ***euch***
er/sie/es/man interessiert ***sich***	*Sie/sie interessieren* ***sich***

Ich interessiere ***mich*** *für die Umwelt.*
I am interested in the environment.

After subordinating conjunctions like ***dass*** (that) and ***weil*** (because), the reflexive pronoun comes after the subject (e.g. *ich, wir*) and the verb goes to the end.

Ich möchte mit Tieren arbeiten, ***weil*** *ich* ***mich*** *für die Umwelt interessiere.*
I want to work with animals because I'm interested in the environment.

4 Rewrite each sentence, putting the words into the correct order.

1 Er sich Freiheit. auf seine freut

....

2 Interessiert euch Computer? ihr für

....

3 Ich Freunden. verstehe sehr mit meinen gut mich

....

H 4 Sie ihrem sich mit unterhalten Lehrer

....

H 5 Wir bei unseren entschuldigen uns Eltern

....

H **Reflexive pronouns** can be in the **accusative** or the **dative** case.

Common verbs that take the **accusative reflexive pronoun** are:

sich interessieren (für) to be interested (in)
sich konzentrieren (auf) to concentrate (on)
sich treffen (mit) to meet
sich entscheiden to decide

Common verbs which take the **dative reflexive pronoun** are:

sich Sorgen machen (um) to worry (about)
sich wünschen to wish
*Ich mache **mir** Sorgen um meine Zukunft.*
I worry about my future.
*Wünschst du **dir** eine bessere Zukunft?*
Do you wish for a better future?

Note that only the ***ich*** and ***du*** forms are different in the **dative** case. They become ***mir*** and ***dir***. All the other dative forms are the same as the accusative forms.

If there is only **one object** in the sentence, the reflexive pronoun will be in the **accusative case**.
*Ich verletze **mich**.* I injure (myself).
If there are **two objects** in the sentence, the reflexive pronoun will be in the dative case.
*Ich verletze mir **die Hand**.* I injure my hand.
Some verbs have a different meaning depending on whether the reflexive pronoun is in the accusative or the dative case, e.g. *sich vorstellen*:
*Ich stelle **mich** vor.* I introduce myself.
*Ich stelle mir **vor**, dass ...* I imagine that ...

H 5 Complete these sentences with the correct form of the reflexive pronoun.

1 Wünscht ihr .... auch Frieden?
2 Ich fürchte .... nicht vor der Zukunft, denn ich habe positive Gedanken.
3 Wir möchten .... zu dieser Frage nicht äußern, da wir die Antwort nicht wissen.
4 Sein Vater sorgt .... um ihn, weil die Konkurrenz in dem Unternehmen wahrscheinlich sehr hoch sein wird.
5 Willst du .... bei einem Unternehmen vorstellen, dessen Beitrag zum Umweltschutz hoch ist?
6 Kannst du .... vorstellen, in einer großen Firma zu arbeiten, deren Büro im Ausland ist?

sich äußern means 'to express yourself'.

das Unternehmen is a synonym for *die Firma*.

dessen and ***deren*** are relative pronouns in the genitive case that mean 'whose' or 'of which'. *dessen* is used for masculine and neuter nouns and *deren* for feminine and plural.

F 6 Translate these sentences into German.

1 I am interested in the training at the company.

....

2 She is looking forward to the conversation with the teacher.

....

3 We sit down and look for a job on the internet.

....

4 He hopes that he earns a lot of money.

....

5 They get on well with their colleagues.

....

H 7 Translate this paragraph into English on a separate sheet.

Ich sorge mich ein bisschen um meine Noten. Ich unterhalte mich oft mit meinen Freunden über unsere Ausbildung. Wir wünschen uns alle, in die Oberstufe zu gehen. Ich interessiere mich für Medien, aber ich bin mir noch nicht sicher, ob ich studieren will. Nach den Prüfungen werde ich aber erst einmal reisen!

2 Was ist dein Traumberuf?

- **F** Using *werden* (to become)
- **F** Forming past participles of *-ieren* verbs

Module 8
Student Book pp. 186–87

1 Complete each sentence using a noun from the box.

Künstler Service Polizistin Ärztin Kellner Bühne Lehrer

1 Joel arbeitet als .... und bedient Menschen in einem Restaurant.

2 Tim und Samira sind Arzt und .... und helfen kranken Menschen.

3 Alina will als .... bei der Polizei arbeiten. Das ist ihr Traum.

4 Elias hat einen Plan: Er will später als .... mit Jugendlichen arbeiten.

5 Paul malt gern und arbeitet als ....

6 Charlotte hat eine Webseite mit einem Reise-.......................................

7 Malik mag Rockmusik, steht oft auf einer .... und singt gern vor vielen Menschen.

Nouns for jobs and roles have ***-in*** at the end of the masculine noun to create a feminine version. Some nouns also add an umlaut in the feminine version.

2 Circle the correct form of *werden* to complete each sentence.

1 Mein Bruder möchte Polizist **wird** / **werden**.

2 Sie **wird** / **werden** Lehrerin von Beruf.

3 Das Wetter **werden** / **wird** immer besser.

4 Möchtet ihr beide Künstler **werdet** / **werden**?

5 Ich will einfach nur ein gutes Einkommen haben und reich **werde** / **werden**!

G

The irregular verb **werden** can be used:

- to form the future tense: *Ich **werde** morgen ins Kino gehen.*
- to mean 'to become' (or 'get/turn into something'):

*Ich will Arzt **werden**.* I want to **become** a doctor.
*Das Essen **wird** kalt.* The food **is getting** cold.
*Die Kinder **werden** müde.* The children **are getting/becoming** tired.

ich werde
du wirst
er/sie/es/man wird
wir werden
ihr werdet
Sie/sie werden

3 Complete these sentences with the past participle of the verb in brackets.

1 Hast du dich heute im Unterricht ....? (*konzentrieren*)

2 Ich habe mich schon immer für einen Job in der Service-Industrie .... (*interessieren*)

3 Die Firma hat mich noch nicht .... (*informieren*)

4 Aus diesem Grund haben die 16-jährigen Schüler mit ihrem Lehrer .... (*diskutieren*)

G

To form the past participle of an ***-ieren*** verb, you don't add *ge-* but you do take off the ***-en*** and add **-t**, as for regular past participles.

infinitive	**past participle**
respektieren	respektier**t**
organisieren	organisier**t**
studieren	studier**t**
akzeptieren	akzeptier**t**
passieren	passier**t**

4 Translate these sentences into German on a separate sheet.

1 She would like to become a German teacher.

2 My parents both studied medicine.

3 He wants to have his own company.

4 We are getting ill.

5 I want to become an artist, but my parents have not accepted that.

2 Was ist dein Traumberuf?

- **H** Revising the conditional and imperfect subjunctive
- **H** Using *werden* in different tenses

H 1 Complete each sentence using a verb from the box.

auftreten gründen träumen wiederholen

If you don't know the meaning of a verb, try to work out the meaning from a noun or similar verbs that you already know.

1 Ich habe den Wunsch, mit meinem Freund erfolgreich eine Firma zu ....

2 Wir .... davon, in die Oberstufe zu gehen.

3 Ich möchte gern Schauspielerin werden und auf einer Bühne ....

4 Ich hoffe darauf, das Schuljahr nicht .... zu müssen.

G Remember that the **conditional** is formed using **würde** + infinitive. *Würde* means 'would'.
Ich ***würde*** *die Gelegenheit nutzen.*
I **would** use the opportunity.
It can also be used with ***gern*** to say what you would like to do.
Wir ***würden gern*** *ein Studium machen.*
We **would like** to do our studies.
Sein and ***haben*** are usually used in the **imperfect subjunctive** to express a conditional idea:
Das ***wäre*** *ein Fehler.* That **would be** a mistake.
Ich ***hätte*** *ein Ziel.* I **would have** a goal.

G The irregular verb ***werden*** can be used to form the future tense and also means 'to become' (or 'get' / 'turn into'):
Das Essen ***wird*** *kalt.* The food **is getting** cold.
Ich ***werde*** *krank.* I am **becoming/getting** ill.
Ich möchte Arzt ***werden****.*
I would like to **become** a doctor.
Werden is also used in past tenses.
Imperfect tense: *Das Essen* ***wurde*** *kalt.*
The food **got** cold (literally 'became cold').
Perfect tense: *Das Essen* ***ist*** *kalt* ***geworden****.*
The food **has got** cold.

H 2 Circle the correct form of the conditional to complete each sentence.

1 Die Firma **würde** / **wäre** / **hätte** sogar 20 Jugendliche ausbilden.

2 Vor allem **würde** / **wäre** / **hätte** ich gern mehrere Kunden.

3 **Würdest** / **Wärst** / **Hättest** du es wagen, ein eigenes Unternehmen zu gründen?

4 Was **würden** / **wären** / **hätten** deine Eltern zu dieser Entscheidung sagen?

5 Tierärztin zu werden **würde** / **wäre** / **hätte** mein Traum!

If there is an infinitive at the end of the sentence, you will need to use a form of *würd-*.

H 3 Complete these sentences with the correct form of *werden*.

1 Meine Geschwister sind vor zwei Jahren beide Polizisten ....

2 Ihr Traum, ein Unternehmen zu gründen, ... letztes Jahr Wirklichkeit.

3 Jedes Jahr .... die Möglichkeiten, einen guten Job zu finden, immer geringer.

4 Leider .... wir keine andere Wahl haben.

H 4 Translate this paragraph into German on a separate sheet.

It is my wish to become a teacher. My brother wants to study medicine. As a doctor, his goal would be to help people. If he avoids mistakes, he will be successful. My sister would start her own company if she had enough money. After school, my father became an actor.

3 Was sind deine Stärken?

Revising subordinating conjunctions

1 Unjumble the letters to rewrite the words correctly. Then translate them into English.

1 aTme ....
2 äSetrk ....
3 täVdnisersn ....
4 scHhhuleoc ....
H 5 iltiietanv ....
H 6 iFehkäitg ....

2 Complete these sentences by translating the verbs in brackets into German, in the correct form.

1 Ich habe viel Verständnis und kann sehr gut .... (*to listen*)
2 Ich bin sehr organisiert und kann gut .... (*to plan*)
3 Ich .... immer die Wahrheit. (*to say*)
4 Ich kann sehr gut .... (*to talk*)
5 Ich .... fast immer. (*to win*)
H 6 Ich kann andere für neue Ideen .... (*to inspire, to be enthusiastic*)

G

Subordinating conjunctions link clauses together and send the verb to the end of the clause.

als when (past) | *ob* whether | *weil* because
dass that | *obwohl* although | *wenn* if, when

Ich war klein. → *Ich wollte Ärztin werden,* ***als*** *ich klein war.*
I wanted to become a doctor, **when** I was little.

When you start with the subordinating conjunction, the verbs of both parts meet in the middle, around a comma. This is called a 'verb-comma-verb' structure.

Als *ich klein war, wollte ich Ärztin werden.*
When I was little, I wanted to become a doctor.

H Other examples of subordinating conjunctions:
seitdem since then, since | *bevor* before
nachdem after | *während* during, while
sobald as soon as

G

You have already seen verbs in the imperfect tense:
Ich ***war*** *sechzehn Jahre alt.* I **was** sixteen years old.
Ich ***hatte*** *einen Job.* I **had** a job.
Es gab *viele Möglichkeiten.* **There were** many opportunities.

You can also use **modal verbs** with an infinitive in the imperfect:
Ich ***wollte*** *in einem Team arbeiten.* I **wanted** to work in a team.
Ich ***musste*** *studieren.* I **had** to study.
Ich ***konnte*** *der Umwelt helfen.* I **could/was able** to help the environment.
Ich ***durfte*** *eine Ausbildung machen.* I **was allowed** to do a training course.

3 Rewrite each sentence, putting the words in the subordinate clause into the correct order.

1 Ich wollte Polizistin werden, *war ich jünger als.*

....

2 Sie will Tierärztin werden, *liebt sie weil Pferde.*

....

3 Man bekommt eine gute Stelle, *lernt man fleißig wenn.*

....

4 Ich kann mich leider nicht verbessern, *ich viel obwohl lerne.*

....

Remember that the subordinating conjunction comes after the comma and sends the verb to the end of the clause.

5 Er sagt, *dass hat er gute viele Ideen.*

....

6 Ich weiß noch nicht, *auf ich Hochschule die ob gehe.*

....

4 Rewrite each sentence, starting with the subordinate clause.

Remember the 'verb-comma-verb' structure.

1 Sie will Künstlerin werden, wenn sie 20 Jahre alt ist.

....

2 Ich habe mich verbessert, als ich viel gelernt habe.

....

3 Meine Eltern waren nie zufrieden, obwohl ich in der Schule immer gut war.

....

4 Ich habe nicht gewusst, dass er so viele Stärken hat.

....

H 5 Ich möchte später Lehrer werden, weil ich gut erklären kann.

....

H 6 Ich bin mir jedoch noch nicht sicher, ob ich einen guten Abschluss haben werde.

....

H 5 On a separate sheet, rewrite each pair of sentences as one, starting with the subordinating conjunction in brackets.

1 Ich lerne nicht mehr so viel. Meine Noten sind nur noch durchschnittlich. (*seitdem*)

Seitdem ich nicht mehr so viel lerne, sind meine Noten nur noch durchschnittlich.

2 Ihr seid mit der Schule fertig. Ihr werdet um die Welt reisen. (*sobald*)

3 Sie hat studiert. Sie hat viel Initiative für die Umwelt gezeigt. (*während*)

4 Ich war mit meinem Studium fertig. Ich habe mir eine Stelle als Arzt gesucht. (*nachdem*)

5 Wir sind auf die Hochschule gegangen. Wir hatten bereits einen Job im Unternehmen. (*bevor*)

6 Ich sehe den Fehler. Ich habe keine Erklärung dafür. (*obwohl*)

F 6 Translate these sentences into English on a separate sheet.

1 Ich bin gut mit Sprachen.

2 Er sagt, dass er gut zuhört.

3 Als ich jünger war, hatte ich mehr Verständnis für andere Menschen.

4 Obwohl ich Tiere liebe, durfte ich als Kind nie ein Pferd haben.

5 Wenn ich mehr Geld habe, werde ich in die schöne Schweiz reisen.

H 7 Translate this paragraph into German on a separate sheet.

Use the imperfect tense of *wollen* to translate 'have wanted'.

Since I was little, I have always wanted to appear on a big stage. As soon as I was old enough, I looked for a job in a theatre. After my school leaving qualification, I started my training there. While I studied at the theatre, I worked with many famous actors.

4 Ein Zwischenjahr? Warum nicht?

Student Book pp. 190–91

F Revising relative clauses • F Asking questions

1 Complete each sentence using a word from the box.

Ende Zukunft Kultur Moment Jahr

> Use the glossary to look up any words that are unfamiliar and try to learn them.

1 Ich möchte ein soziales .... im Ausland machen.

2 Ich plane meine .... im Umweltschutz, weil ich die Natur liebe.

3 Im .... weiß ich noch nicht, ob ich mit jüngeren oder älteren Menschen arbeite.

4 Am .... ist jede Erfahrung wichtig, weil man überall etwas lernt.

5 Ich möchte die österreichische .... kennenlernen, weil mein Freund aus Österreich kommt.

> **G** Remember that **relative pronouns** (*der, die, das, die* – who, which, that) refer back to someone or something. They send the verb to the end of the clause, and they always follow a comma.
> *ein Job,* ***der*** *mir Freude bringt*
> a job **which** brings me joy

> **G** Remember that there are two ways to form a question in German.
> - Invert the **verb** and the subject of the sentence: ***Warst*** *du im Ausland?*
> - Use a **question word**: ***Wo*** *warst du?*

2 Complete these sentences with the correct relative pronoun.

1 Ich will in meinem sozialen Jahr eine Reise machen, ... spannend ist.

2 Ich möchte in meinem sozialen Jahr Essen probieren, ... ich noch nicht kenne.

3 Er ist ein Mensch, ... nicht gern auf eine Bühne tritt.

4 Ich möchte Kulturen kennenlernen, ... mir bis jetzt noch fremd sind.

5 Ich will sicherlich keinen Job haben, ... hart ist, denn ich will glücklich sein.

3 Rewrite each question, putting the words into the correct order.

> *genommen* and *gestanden* are the past participles of *nehmen* and *stehen*.

1 soziales willst dein machen Wo du Jahr?

....

2 du als genommen Schüler einen Job Hast? ....

3 Sie gestanden einer einmal schon auf Haben Bühne? ....

4 bedeutet Bildung Was eine für dich gute? ....

5 nimmst Jahr du im Job Welchen sozialen? ....

4 Translate these sentences into German on a separate sheet.

1 Next year I'm doing a social year.

2 I want to help people who are ill.

3 Do you have a job that you like?

4 I am very interested in Austrian food.

5 In the end, my social year was a very positive experience.

4 Ein Zwischenjahr? Warum nicht?

H Using adjectives as nouns

H 1 Complete these sentences by translating the words in brackets into German.

1 Mein soziales Jahr ist sehr .... und hat mir bisher sehr gutgetan. (*interesting*)

2 Es ist nicht ...., einen Job mit einem guten Einkommen zu finden. (*easy*)

3 Ich lege großen Wert darauf, mal eine .... Erfahrung machen zu können. (*other*)

4 Jene Kollegen behandeln mich gut und sind sehr .... (*nice, kind*)

5 Ich erwarte sehr .... Gutes von meinem sozialen Jahr. (*a lot of*)

G

H Adjectives can be used as a **noun** after *etwas* (something), *nichts* (nothing), *viel* (a lot, much), *wenig* (little) and *alles* (everything). Just add a capital letter and an ending.

- After *etwas, nichts, viel, wenig*, add **-es**:

***Etwas Nettes** ist passiert.*
Something nice happened.
*Es lag **nichts Neues** auf dem Tisch.*
There was nothing new (lying) on the table.
*Er hat **viel Gutes** getan.* He did a lot of good.

- After *alles*, the ending is -*e*.

***Alles Gute** zum Geburtstag!*
All the best on your birthday!

- You can also use the **comparative form** of the adjective together with ***als***:

*Es gibt **nichts Besseres** als ...*
There is **nothing better** than ...
*Es gibt **viel Interessanteres** als ...*
There are many **more interesting** things than ...

H 2 Circle the correct adjectival noun to complete each sentence.

1 Ich möchte ihm etwas **Nützliches** / **Nützliche** für sein soziales Jahr schenken.

2 Es gibt nichts **Schwierigeres** / **Schwieriger** in dieser Phase als feste Pläne zu machen.

3 Die Hochschulbildung in diesem Land ist alles **Anderes** / **Andere** als gut.

4 Es ist eine Tatsache, dass er im sozialen Jahr viel **Interessantes** / **Interessante** gelernt hat.

5 Er besitzt viele Kenntnisse und an seiner Rede kann ich nur wenig **Schlechtes** / **Schlechte** finden.

6 Zum Glück ist nichts **Schlimmes** / **Schlimme** passiert!

H 3 Complete these sentences by translating the words in brackets into German.

1 Ich möchte in meinem sozialen Jahr .... machen. (*something easy*)

2 Mein soziales Jahr war langweilig und ich habe .... gelernt. (*little new*)

3 Ich kann mir .... vorstellen als nach meinem Abschluss zu reisen. (*nothing more lovely*)

4 Im sozialen Jahr kann man gesellschaftlich .... tun. (*much useful*)

5 Es hat mir große Freude gemacht, ... kennenzulernen. (*everything foreign*)

H 4 Translate this paragraph into German on a separate sheet.

I'm already really looking forward to my social year. I would like to do something interesting and achieve something socially useful. I think there's nothing better than helping other people. Therefore, I'm intending to work in a hospital. After that, I can decide what I want to study.

5 Meine Träume für die Zukunft

Dealing with unfamiliar vocabulary • Using *hoffen aus* and *hoffen*, dass

1 Draw lines to match up the German words with their English translations.

1 Rolle	**a** colleague
2 Chef	**b** partner
3 Kollegin	**c** support
4 Partner	**d** circle of friends
H **5** Freundeskreis	**e** role
H **6** Gegenwart	**f** present
H **7** Unterstützung	**g** boss

2 Complete each sentence using a verb from the box.

vorbereiten   heiraten   geben   liefern   bringen

1 In der Zukunft wird es doppelt so viele interessante Jobs wie jetzt ....

2 Was wird uns die Zukunft ....?

3 Wir hoffen, dass wir nette Partner finden und später vielleicht auch ....

H **4** In der Zukunft werden vielleicht Computer, die allein fahren, das Essen zu uns nach Hause ....

H **5** Wir müssen uns alle für unsere Zukunft gut ....

G

The verb **hoffen** can be used in different ways:

- *Ich* ***hoffe auf*** + accusative noun (I'm **hoping for** ...)

Ich ***hoffe auf*** *einen guten Job.*

- *Ich* ***hoffe, dass*** ... (I **hope that** ...)

Remember that *dass* sends the verb to the end of the clause.

Ich ***hoffe, dass*** *die Arbeit interessant ist.*

Ich ***hoffe, dass*** *ich eine interessante Arbeit finde.*

H *Ich* ***hoffe, dass*** *ich eine interessante Arbeit finden werde.*

G

There are a number of ways to work out the meaning of words you have not seen before:

- Look for cognates and **near-cognates** (words that look very similar to English words): e.g. *r**u**nd* (r**ou**nd), ***K**on**z**entration* (**c**on**c**entration), *Fa**k**tor* (fa**c**tor.) But be careful of 'false friends': e.g. *Chef* (boss, not chef), H *bald* (soon, not bald).
- Break **compound nouns** into words you know: e.g. *Zahnarzt*: *Zahn* + *Arzt* (tooth + doctor – dentist).
- Use the **context** to work out the meaning.
- Use **word families** to help you: e.g. *das Drittel* (third) – *drei* (three); H *prüfen* (to test, examine) – *die Prüfung* (exam, test); H *zählen* (to count) – *die Zahl* (number).

3 Complete these sentences by translating the phrases in brackets into German. Use the correct form of *hoffen* and *auf* + noun or *dass* + clause.

1 Ich hoffe auf .... (*a wonderful partner*)

2 Er hofft, dass .... (*he passes the exam*)

3 Wir hoffen auf .... (*a job abroad*)

4 Sie hofft, dass .... (*she studies medicine*)

5 Ihr hofft auf .... (*an exciting social year*)

4 Rewrite each sentence, using *hoffen* + *auf*/*dass* as indicated.

> Remember that the subordinate clauses that follow *dass* will need a verb, which needs to be at the end of the clause.

1 Wir hoffen auf eine glückliche Zukunft.

Wir hoffen, dass ....

2 Sie hofft, dass sie viele gute Chancen im Leben hat.

Sie hofft auf ....

3 Ich hoffe auf einen freundlichen Chef und nette Kollegen in meiner Ausbildung.

Ich hoffe, dass ....

H 4 Die Mehrheit der Schüler hofft, dass sie einen Job im Umweltschutz finden wird.

Die Mehrheit der Schüler hofft auf ....

H 5 Er hat noch Zweifel, aber er hofft trotzdem auf gute Noten und einen guten Abschluss.

Er hat noch Zweifel, aber er hofft trotzdem, dass ....

H 5 Complete these German sentences using *ich hoffe auf* and *ich hoffe, dass,* and the ideas in brackets.

1 (*have a successful higher education*)

Ich hoffe auf ....

Ich hoffe, dass ....

2 (*get support from my family*)

Ich hoffe auf ....

Ich hoffe, dass ....

3 (*learn many new skills*)

Ich hoffe auf ....

Ich hoffe, dass ....

F 6 Translate these sentences into German.

1 He would like to work abroad. ....

2 We want an interesting job and a good income.

....

3 I hope to have a big family. ....

4 She hopes for lots of new friends at university.

....

5 Marriage is not so important to me. ....

H 7 Translate this paragraph into English on a separate sheet.

Ich muss mich bald entscheiden, was ich in der Zukunft machen will. Ich hoffe auf Unterstützung von meinem Freundeskreis. Ich hoffe auch, dass ich in den Prüfungen gute Noten bekomme. Ich brauche einen guten Abschluss, um auf die Universität zu gehen. Ich möchte einen Job, wo ich etwas Gutes tun kann.

Glossary

bold = this word will appear in Higher exams only

Abschluss (m)	*leaving qualification*
Alltag (m)	*daily routine, everyday life*
anziehen; (sich) anziehen	*(to) put on, attract, get (oneself) dressed | putting on, attracting, getting (oneself) dressed*
Arbeit (f)	*work, test, employment*
arbeiten	*(to) work | working*
Arzt (m)	*doctor*
Ärztin (f)	*doctor*
ausbilden	*(to) train, educate*
Ausbildung (f)	*training, education*
aussehen	*(to) look, appear | looking, appearing*
außerdem	*moreover, besides, in addition*
äußern; (sich) äußern	*(to) express (oneself)*
bedeuten	*(to) mean | meaning*
bedienen	*(to) serve | serving*
begeistern	*(to) inspire, be enthusiastic*
behandeln	*(to) treat*
beide	*both*
Beitrag (m)	*contribution*
bereit	*ready*
bereits	*already*
Beruf (m)	*occupation, job, profession*
beruflich	*professional, professionally, vocational, vocationally*
besitzen	*(to) own*
bevor	*before*
bisher	*until now*
bringen	*(to) bring | bringing*
Bühne (f)	*stage*
Chance (f)	*chance*
Chef/Chefin (m/f)	*boss, head, leader*
da	*since, because, there*
dessen, deren	*whose*
doppelt	*double, twice*
Drittel (nt)	*third*
durchschnittlich	*(on) average*
einfach	*easy, easily, simple, simply, single (ticket)*
Einkommen (nt)	*income, pay*
Ende (nt); am Ende	*end; in the end*
entscheiden	*(to) decide*
Entscheidung (f)	*decision*
entschuldigen; (sich) entschuldigen	*(to) apologise, excuse*
Erfahrung (f)	*experience*
erfolgreich	*successful, successfully*
erklären	*(to) explain*
Erklärung (f)	*explanation*
erwarten	*(to) expect*
etwas (Nettes)	*something (nice)*
Euro (m)	*euro*
Fähigkeit (f)	*skill, ability, capability*
Faktor (m)	*factor*
Fall (m)	*case*
Fehler (m)	*mistake, error*
fertig	*ready, finished*
Firma (f)	*firm, company, business*

Firmen (pl)	*firms, companies*
fremd	*strange, strangely, foreign*
freuen; (sich) freuen (über); sich freuen auf	*(to) be happy (about), make happy, please | being happy (about), making happy, pleasing; (to) look forward to | looking forward to*
Frieden (m)	*peace*
fürchten; sich fürchten vor	*(to) fear; (to) be afraid of*
geben	*(to) give | giving*
(aux) ... gedacht	*thought / (have, has) thought*
Gedanke (m)	*thought*
Gegenwart (f)	*present*
Geld (nt)	*money*
Gelegenheit (f)	*opportunity*
genauso	*just as*
(aux) ... genommen	*took / (have, has) taken*
gering	*low, small*
gesellschaftlich	*social, socially*
Gespräch (nt)	*conversation*
(aux) ... gestanden	*stood / (have, has) stood*
(aux) ... getan	*did, put / (has, have) done, put*
gewinnen	*(to) win | winning*
(aux) ... gewusst	*knew / (has, have) known*
gleich	*same, right away, just, immediately, equal*
gleichzeitig	*at the same time*
glücklich	*happy, happily, fortunate*
Grund (m)	*reason*
gründen	*(to) start, found*

hart	*hard*
heiraten	*(to) get married, marry | getting married, marrying*
heraus	*out, outside*
Hilfe (f)	*help*
Hochschulbildung (f)	*higher education*
Hochschule (f)	*college, university*
hoffen	*(to) hope | hoping*
Idee (f)	*idea*
Industrie (f)	*industry*
Initiative (f)	*initiative*
...jährig	*years (old)*
jedoch	*however*
jene(r)	*that, those*
Job (m)	*job*
jünger	*younger*
Kenntnis (f)	*knowledge*
knapp	*scarce, in short supply*
Kollege (m)	*colleague*
Kollegin (f)	*colleague*
Konkurrenz (f)	*competition*
Kontakt (m)	*contact*
Konzentration (f)	*concentration*
krank	*ill, sick*
Kreis (m)	*circle, district*
Kunde (m)	*customer*
Kundin (f)	*customer*
lag	*(I, she, he, it) lay, was situated*
legen	*(to) lay, put | laying, putting*
Lehrer/Lehrerin (m/f)	*teacher*
leisten	*(to) achieve, perform, do*
liefern	*(to) deliver, supply*

Lust (f)	*desire*
Medizin (f)	*medicine*
mehrere	*several, various*
Mehrheit (f)	*majority*
Möglichkeit (f)	*possibility*
Moment (m); im Moment	*moment; at the moment*
nachdem	*after*
neu	*new*
nimmst	*(you (sing informal)) take | are taking*
noch	*still, yet, nor, another, ... else*
Note (f)	*grade, note*
ob	*whether, if*
Oberstufe (f)	*sixth form, college*
obwohl	*although*
ohne; **ohne ... zu (+ infinitive)**	*without; without (+ verb)*
österreichisch	*Austrian*
Partner/Partnerin (m/f)	*partner*
Pferd (nt)	*horse*
pflegen	*to care (for)*
Phase (f)	*phase*
Plan (m)	*plan*
planen	*(to) plan | planning*
Polizei (f)	*police*
Polizist/Polizistin (m/f)	*police officer*
präsentieren	*(to) present, show | presenting, showing*
Prozent (nt)	*percent*
prüfen	*(to) test, examine, check*
Prüfung (f)	*exam*
Rede (f)	*speech*
reden	*(to) talk*
reich	*rich*
Rolle (f)	*role*
rund	*round, around*
sagen	*(to) say, tell | saying, telling*
schenken	*(to) give (as a present)*
schon	*already*
schön	*lovely, beautiful, beautifully*
Schutz (m)	*protection*
seitdem	*since then, since*
selbst, selber	*self*
Service (m)	*service*
setzen, sich setzen; sich hinsetzen	*(to) set, place, put | setting, placing, putting; (to) sit down | sitting down*
sich	*herself, himself, itself, oneself, yourself (formal), themselves, yourselves (formal) (reflex) / each other (recip)*
sich sorgen (um)	*(to) worry, care (about)*
sicher	*safe, safely, sure, surely, certain, certainly*
sicherlich	*certainly*
sitzen bleiben	*to repeat a year in school*
sobald	*as soon as*
sogar	*even*
sogenannt	*so-called*
sonst	*otherwise, else*
Stärke (f)	*strength*
Start (m)	*start*
statt ... zu (+ infinitive)	*instead of (+ verb)*
stehen	*(to) stand | standing*
Stelle (f)	*workplace, position, job*

		😐	🙂	😎
studieren	*(to) study (at university) / studying (at university)*			
Studium (nt)	*studies*			
Suche (f)	*search*			
suchen	*(to) look for, seek / looking for, seeking*			
Tatsache (f)	*fact*			
Team (nt)	*team*			
Traum (m)	*dream*			
träumen	*(to) dream*			
treten (auf)	*(to) step (on) / stepping (on)*			
tritt	*(she, he, it, one) steps (on) / is stepping (on)*			
unbedingt	*absolutely*			
Universität (f)/ Uni	*university*			
unmöglich	*impossible*			
unterhalten; (sich) unterhalten	*(to) amuse oneself, chat*			
Unternehmen (nt)	*company, enterprise, business*			
Unterstützung (f)	*support*			
verbessern; (sich) verbessern	*(to) improve, make better, get better / improving, making better, getting better*			
verdienen	*(to) earn, deserve / earning, deserving*			
verschieden	*different, diverse*			
Verständnis (nt)	*understanding*			
verstehen; sich verstehen mit	*(to) understand / understanding; (to) get on with / getting on with*			
vor allem	*above all*			
vorbereiten	*(to) prepare*			
vorhaben	*(to) intend, plan*			
vorschlagen	*(to) suggest*			
vorstellen; (sich) vorstellen	*(to) introduce (oneself), imagine*			
Vorstellung (f)	*performance, idea, introduction*			
wagen	*(to) dare, risk / daring, risking*			
Wahl (f)	*choice*			
wahrscheinlich	*probably*			
weiß	*(I) know (something) / (she, he, it, one) knows (something)*			
weiter	*further*			
wert	*worth*			
wiederholen	*(to) repeat*			
Wunsch (m)	*wish, desire*			
wünschen, sich wünschen	*to want, wish*			
wurde	*(I, she, he, it) became*			
zählen	*(to) count*			
Ziel (nt)	*destination, goal*			
zuhören	*(to) listen*			
Zweifel (m)	*doubt*			

Foundation translation revision

German to English

1 Rewrite each English translation, putting the words into the correct order.

1 Ich möchte gern Künstler werden. *artist become I like an would to*

....

2 Ich habe meinen Koffer vergessen. *forgotten I suitcase have my*

....

3 Wir haben in einem Doppelzimmer geschlafen. *slept double room We in a*

....

4 Ich interessiere mich für die Berge und die Küste. *interested in coast mountains am and the I the*

....

5 Alle Menschen sollen die Umwelt schützen. *environment protect Everybody should the*

....

2 Draw lines to match up the German sentences with their English translations.

1 Ich möchte gern Polizistin werden.
2 Die Ärztin hat ihre Tasche vergessen.
3 Wir haben in einem Zelt geschlafen.
4 Ich interessiere mich für fremde Kulturen.
5 Alle Menschen sollen Glas recyceln.

a Everybody should recycle glass.
b I am interested in foreign cultures.
c The doctor forgot her bag.
d We slept in a tent.
e I would like to become a police officer.

3 Underline the mistake(s) in the English translations and write out the translations correctly.

1 Ich möchte Lehrer werden. *I would like to be a teacher.*

....

2 Ich habe meinen Koffer verloren. *I have lost my bag.*

....

3 Wir haben an der Küste gezeltet. *We camped in the mountains.*

....

4 Ich interessiere mich sehr für Tiere. *I am very interested in the weather.*

....

5 Man soll Papier sammeln. *We should recycle paper.*

....

4 Translate these sentences into English on a separate sheet.

1 Ich möchte Ärztin werden.
2 Ich habe meine Tasche verloren.
3 Wir haben auf einem Berg gezeltet.
4 Ich interessiere mich sehr für die Umwelt.
5 Wir sollen Glas sammeln und recyceln.

English to German

1 Colour one box from each column to translate each sentence into German. Use a different colour for each sentence. Then write out your translations.

Ich werde	auf eine	in Berlin	gegangen.
Wir sind	im Team	Einkommen	sehr wichtig.
Ich warte	ein gutes	ist für mich	im Geschäft.
Die Arbeit	durfte	ins Museum	haben.
Ich	gestern	freie Stelle	studieren.

1 I will have a good income. ....

2 We went to the museum yesterday. ....

3 I am waiting for a free position in the shop. ....

4 Working in a team is very important to me. ....

5 I was allowed to study in Berlin. ....

2 Complete each German translation using a word from the box.

Stelle Schloss Besuch Tisch Projekt

1 I will reserve a table at the restaurant. — *Ich werde einen .... im Restaurant reservieren.*

2 We worked on the project as a team. — *Wir haben als Team an dem .... gearbeitet.*

3 I am looking forward to my visit to the company. — *Ich freue mich auf meinen .... in der Firma.*

4 A position at the university is quite important to me. — *Eine .... an der Universität ist mir ziemlich wichtig.*

5 I was allowed to visit the castle. — *Ich durfte das .... besuchen.*

3 Complete these sentences by translating the words in brackets into German.

1 Ich .... (*will*) in einem Team .... (*work*).

2 Er hat .... (*the university*) .... (*visited*).

3 Ich .... (*am looking forward to*) unser Doppelzimmer .... (*with a bathroom*).

4 Ein guter Job ist .... (*very important to me*).

5 Ich .... (*was allowed*) im Museum nicht laut .... (*speak*).

4 Translate these sentences into German on a separate sheet.

1 I will visit the beautiful museum.

2 We reserved a double room with a bathroom.

3 I am looking forward to working in a team.

4 A good income is very important to me.

5 She was allowed to go to university.

Higher translation revision

German to English

1 Circle the odd one out.

1 Unternehmen / Ausflug / Stelle / Firma
2 Note / Oberstufe / Umwelt / Abschluss
3 bereit / wünschen / kämpfen / reisen
4 hätte / welche / würde / wäre
5 nützlich / toll / beenden / verschieden
6 nachdem / sobald / seitdem / danach

2 Complete these sentences by translating the words in brackets into English.

1 ....(*Nachdem ich*) have finished university, ...(*werde ich*) look for a job ....(*in einem großen Unternehmen*).

2 ....(*Ich wünsche mir*) a job with a lot of ....(*Verantwortung*).

3 I would like to do ....(*etwas Nützliches für die Gesellschaft*) and to fight against ....(*Klimawandel*).

4 I am ready ....(*ein soziales Jahr zu machen*).

5 ....(*Welche Firma*) will you choose?

3 Correct the English translation by crossing through the incorrect word(s) and writing the correction above it.

Sobald ich meinen Abschluss habe, werde ich ins Ausland reisen. Ich möchte fremde Länder sehen und etwas Tolles erleben. Ich würde gern um die ganze Welt fliegen, aber das ist zu teuer. Und es ist auch nicht gut für die Umwelt und den Klimawandel. Danach bin ich bereit, in einem Unternehmen zu arbeiten. Welche Zukunft siehst du für dich?

After I have my leaving qualification, I will travel abroad. I want to see foreign countries and do something useful. I would like to travel around the whole world, but that is too expensive. And it is also not good for the pollution and climate change. After that, I am ready to work in a school. Which future do you see for me?

4 Translate this paragraph into English on a separate sheet.

Nachdem ich die Oberstufe beendet habe, werde ich ein soziales Jahr machen. Ich wünsche mir eine bessere Gesellschaft und möchte etwas Nützliches tun. Ich würde gern in einem Unternehmen arbeiten, das gegen den Klimawandel kämpft. Ich bin bereit, für eine bessere Zukunft zu arbeiten. Welchen Weg wirst du nach deinem Abschluss gehen?

English to German

1 Match up the English words/phrases with their German translations. Write the correct letter.

1 sixth form .....
2 earbuds .....
3 state/condition .....
4 credit card .....
5 hotel employee .....
6 double room .....
7 loss .....

a die Kreditkarte
b der Zustand
c das Doppelzimmer
d die Oberstufe
e der Verlust
f die Ohrhörer
g der Hotelmitarbeiter / die Hotelmitarbeiterin

2 Complete each German translation using a word from the box.

lernen übernachten würde verloren

1 Recently I lost my credit card.	*Neulich habe ich meine Kreditkarte ....*
2 We always spend the night at this hotel.	*Wir .... immer in diesem Hotel.*
3 I would like to reserve a double room.	*Ich .... gern ein Doppelzimmer reservieren.*
4 I had to learn a lot in sixth form.	*Ich musste in der Oberstufe viel ....*

3 Translate the sentences into German, using the first letter of each word to help you.

1 I forgot my earbuds.

I ____ h ____ m ____ O ____ v ____.

2 The loss of the employee was difficult.

D ____ V ____ d ____ M ____ w ____ s ____.

3 I would like to do my leaving qualification soon.

I ____ w ____ g ____ b ____ m ____ A ____ m ____.

4 We spent the night in a double room.

W ____ h ____ i ____ e ____ D ____ ü ____.

5 Despite the bad condition of the hotel, we had fun.

T ____ d ____ s ____ Z ____ d ____ H ____ h ____ w ____ S ____.

4 Translate this paragraph into German on a separate sheet.

Recently I spent the night with friends in a hotel. The room was in quite a bad condition and I lost my earbuds. But the employees were very nice. Despite the loss, we had a lot of fun. I would like to go to sixth form and I therefore need to learn now for my leaving qualification.

Vocabulary learning strategies

In the examination you will be tested on your knowledge of German vocabulary, so learning the vocabulary is really important. But how do you make it stick? Here are some strategies you could try.

1 Look, cover, write, check

- Make a list of German words with their English translations.
- Cover either the German list or the English list and write out the English or German translation. Then uncover the first list and check your translation.
- Repeat until you feel confident that you know the words.

2 Create your own flashcards

- Make a set of flashcards with the German on one side and the English on the other. Remember to include *der*, *die* or *das* with nouns so that you learn their gender.
- Pull out cards at random to see if you can remember what the words mean.
- Make a pile of words you know and another pile of words you don't know.
- Keep turning over the flashcards until you remember all of them.

3 Record on a device

Some learners find it helpful to say the words out loud and listen back to them.

- Record yourself on your phone or your device saying the words in both languages.
- Now listen back to the words. Which ones did you remember and which need more practice?
- Record the words again, focusing on those you're finding it difficult to remember.

4 Ask someone else to test you

It's useful to get someone to test you, especially if it's a friend who is also learning the same vocabulary.

- Give your partner a list in both languages of the words you need to learn.
- Ask them to test you on the words both ways: German to English, and English to German.

Testing them on the vocabulary can also help you as you're seeing the words too.

5 Place sticky notes around the room

- Choose a list of words that you want to learn and write each word on a sticky note.
- Place the sticky notes in a place that you often see, such as the fridge or a door. Every time you see the notes, say the German words out loud.
- As you learn each word, replace it with a new sticky note for a different word.

6 Blurt it out and write it down

- Using the Student Book, read through the vocabulary list for a unit.
- Close your book and say out loud all the words you can remember, then write them down.
- Now look back at the list and write the words you didn't know in a different colour.
- Repeat the process until you know all the words.

Use these strategies to help you organise vocabulary and work out meanings.

1 Synonyms and antonyms

It's useful to learn words in pairs of:

- **synonyms** (words that mean the same thing) *schwer* (difficult), *schwierig* (difficult)
- **antonyms** (words that mean the opposite). *billig* (cheap), *teuer* (expensive)

Make a list of pairs of common synonyms and antonyms and add to it as you learn more.

2 Cognates and false friends

- **Cognates** are words that mean the same in both German and English. Start an ongoing list of cognates. *der Sport* sport…
- **False friends** are words that look the same in German and English but mean different things. Create a list of common false friends to avoid falling into traps. *der Chef* boss, head, leader…

3 Prefixes and suffixes

Start an ongoing list of words with common prefixes and suffixes, and learn them together.

- **Prefixes** come at the start of words. Often prefixes are prepositions.

  Prefix: *Haupt-* main → *der Hauptbahnhof* main station

- **Suffixes** come at the end of words. Recognising common ones can help to unlock the meaning of words. For example, ***-ung*** and ***-er*** are often added to verb stems to make them nouns:

reservieren → *die Reservier**ung*** booking, reservation | *malen* → *der Mal**er*** painter

4 Word families

Organising vocabulary into topics can make it easier to remember and use in context. Learning associated words as word families is also useful.

Create a mind-map for a root word and all the words that can be linked to it. Then learn all the words together.

This will help you work out the meaning of unfamiliar words, as you will be able to link them to other words or a family of words.

lieb (*kind, good*)
- die Liebe (*love*)
- lieben (*to love*)
- Lieblings- (prefix) (*favourite*)
- Lieblingsbuch (*favourite book*)

5 Working out genders

In order to be able to use words in sentences, we have to learn the genders. Sometimes you can work out the gender of a word by following patterns. For example:

- all words ending in *-ung*, *-heit* or *-keit* are feminine
- all words ending in *-chen* are neuter.

6 Compound nouns

Use your knowledge of nouns, verbs and adjectives to help you work out the meaning of each part of a compound word.

das Kleidungsgeschäft → *Kleidung* clothes + *Geschäft* shop → clothes shop

A compound noun always takes the gender of the final noun in a compound noun.

Translation strategies: German to English

Here are some useful strategies to help you translate from German into English.

Reading for gist

When you are faced with a passage or sentence to translate from German into English, it is really important to read it through to establish the general meaning, even if you know that there are some words you don't recognise or cannot immediately translate.

Word order

German word order can be very different from English. Before translating, read carefully to the end of each sentence or clause to make sure you take all parts of it into account when pinning down the meaning.

Remember that there are three types of word order in German:

Normal word order

1 *Ich esse oft Gemüse.*

This is normal word order, though slightly different from English: we would translate this as 'I often eat vegetables', rather than 'I eat often vegetables'.

Inverted word order

2 *Ab und zu esse ich Gemüse.*

In this sentence, the subject and verb are inverted after the time phrase at the start. Translating word for word, would give 'Now and again eat I vegetables'. But in English we would say 'Now and again I eat vegetables'.

Word order with subordinate clauses

3 *Am Wochenende essen wir Gemüse, weil mein Vater kocht.*

The verb is sent to the end of the clause after a subordinating conjunction (*weil*). Look out for the comma in German, here indicating a separation between two clauses: 'At the weekend we eat vegetables because my father cooks.'

Bear in mind the major word order switch that occurs when the sentence starts with a sub-clause: *Wenn mein Vater kocht, essen wir immer Gemüse.* Look out for the 'verb-comma-verb' structure as a clue to this: 'When my father cooks, we always eat vegetables.'

Using familiar language, cognates and context

Use familiar language, cognates and context to decode the meaning of unknown words:

Die Band hat ein Konzert im Stadion gegeben.

You can probably work out the (near-)cognates *Band* (band), *Konzert* (concert) and *Stadion* (stadium). You may also know that *gegeben* is the past participle of *geben* (to give), so you understand that the band gave a concert in the stadium.

Gestern sind wir mit der Straßenbahn bis zum Obstgarten gefahren.

In this sentence, you may know *gestern* (yesterday), *mit* (with) and *sind wir gefahren* (we travelled). You may also know *bis* (up to) and *zu* (to).

For *Straßenbahn*, use the context to make an informed guess. It must be some sort of means of transport, as travel is involved. You know that *Straße* is 'street' and *Bahn* is 'railway', so *Straßenbahn* is literally 'street railway': tram.

The same applies to *Obstgarten*. You may know that *Obst* is 'fruit' and *Garten* is 'garden'. So, *Obstgarten* (literally 'fruit garden') is 'orchard'.

Tricky words and false friends

- Look out for relative clauses (see page 45): relative pronouns (such as *der, die, das*) are not translated as 'the', even though they look similar to the definite article:

  Ich habe einen Bruder, ***der*** *Max heißt.* I have a brother **who** is called Max.

  Ich mag den Hund, ***den*** *wir im Park sehen.* I like the dog **which** we see in the park.
- Cognates and near-cognates can help you, but watch out for 'false friends': German words which look similar to English, but have totally different meanings.

  bekommen to receive, get (**not** 'to become')
  fast almost, nearly (**not** 'fast')

Grammar

- Use **tense indicators** and your grammatical knowledge to help you translate the tense:

  Present: ***Heute*** *fahre ich in die Stadt.* **Today** I am going into town.

  Past: ***Letzte Woche*** *sind wir nach Hamburg gefahren.* **Last week** we went to Hamburg.

  Future: ***Nächsten Samstag*** *werden wir nach Wien fahren.* **Next Saturday** we will go to Vienna.
- You can translate some tenses in more than one way. Decide which sounds better in the context:

  Present: *Ich* ***spiele*** *Tennis.* → I play / am playing tennis.

  Perfect: *Ich* ***habe*** *Tennis* ***gespielt****.* → I played / have played tennis.

  Imperfect: *Ich* ***spielte*** *Tennis.* → I played / was playing / used to play tennis.
- Try to spot infinitives at the end of sentences or clauses. Infinitives are likely to occur in future tense sentences or in sentences where there is a modal verb:

  Ich ***werde*** *ein Instrument* ***spielen****.* I **will play** an instrument.

  Wir ***möchten*** *Käse* ***essen****.* We **would like to eat** cheese.
- Look out for small words that make a difference to the meaning, such as *gern, nicht* and *kein*:

  Ich gehe ***gern*** *in die Stadt.* I **like** going into town.

  Ich gehe ***nicht*** *in die Stadt.* I'm **not** going into town.

  Ich habe ***keine*** *Schwester.* I **don't** have a sister.
- Umlauts can also change meaning: *schon* = already, *sch**ö**n* = beautiful

  Look out for these in comparatives (*groß – größer*) and plurals (*Arzt – Ärzte*).
- Split long, compound words up into their various parts to work out the meaning:

  Hauptrolle: Haupt (main) + *Rolle* (role) → main role

Translation skills

- Don't always try to translate word for word. You won't always find that one word in German means one word in English, or vice versa. Similarly, singular nouns in German might equate to plural nouns in English, or vice versa:

  Ich habe meine ***Hausaufgaben*** *gemacht.* I have done my **homework**.
- Don't be afraid to use different words or a different number of words to get a good translation. However, don't stray too far from the meaning or make random guesses.
- It is important to account for every word in a translation, even if some words don't need translating or if you need to add words for the sentence to make sense. For example:

  Montags spielen wir Fußball. **On** Mondays we play football.

  Ich freue mich auf ***die*** *Schule.* I'm looking forward to school.
- It is a good idea to read your translation back to yourself (out loud if you can) to check that it makes sense and sounds natural in English.

Translation strategies: English to German

Here are some strategies for when you are translating from English into German. You will need to draw on your knowledge of German grammar and vocabulary, just as for any other writing task.

Reading for gist

When you have a passage or sentence to translate into German, read the whole thing through once to get the gist. Then work phrase by phrase. Be systematic, and check as you are writing: verb forms, tenses, word order, adjective endings, singular and plural nouns, prepositions and cases.

Grammar

- Look out for **tense triggers** in the English, to make sure you have identified which tense to use in German:

  Yesterday I went to the supermarket. → past (perfect) tense needed

  Tomorrow I will go to school. → future tense needed

  Think carefully about the German verb forms, check your endings and make sure you have put the infinitive or past participle (if there is one) in the right place. For the perfect tense, check you have used the correct auxiliary verb.
- Look out for verbs that are **reflexive** or **separable** in German because these aren't always obvious from the English. Make sure you put the reflexive pronoun or separable prefix in the right place in the sentence:

  In the mornings I exercise. *Morgens **bewege** ich **mich**.*

  After that I watch TV. *Danach **sehe** ich **fern**.*
- **H** Remember that to say you have been doing something for a certain length of time, you use ***seit*** + the present tense. *Seit* takes the dative, so make sure you put the dative ending onto a plural noun that follows it:

  I **have been learning** German for three years. *Ich **lerne seit** drei Jahre**n** Deutsch.*
- Remember the three key **imperfect** tense forms, a simple way of expressing the past:

  I **was** ill. — *Ich **war** krank.*

  We **had** a lot of homework. — *Wir **hatten** viele Hausaufgaben.*

  There was nothing to eat. — ***Es gab** nichts zu essen.*
- You may have to use **modal verbs**, so look out for 'can', 'must', 'should', 'want' and 'allowed to', and remember to send the infinitive to the end of the clause:

  I'm not **allowed** to go to the cinema today. *Ich **darf** heute nicht ins Kino gehen.*

  Look out also for 'could', 'had to', 'was allowed to' and 'wanted', which mean you need to use modal verbs in the imperfect tense:

  As a child, I **wanted** to become a police officer. *Als Kind **wollte** ich Polizist werden.*
- Watch out for 'would' in English. This indicates that you need to use the **conditional** in German, often in the form of *ich möchte*:

  I **would like** to travel. — *Ich **möchte** reisen. / Ich **würde gern** reisen.*

  H or as *ich würde* + infinitive:

  I **would** never **go** hiking. — *Ich **würde** nie wandern **gehen**.*

Time phrases and useful little words

- Learn time and frequency phrases such as last week (*letzte Woche*), next weekend (*nächstes Wochenende*), sometimes (*manchmal*), normally (*normalerweise*), etc.
- Build up a bank of intensifiers, such as *wirklich, echt, ziemlich*, etc.

Endings

- Learn the case endings for articles, possessive adjectives, adjectives and pronouns. Think systematically about which case is required: look for prepositions that trigger certain cases, check subjects and objects. And don't forget to use a capital letter for all nouns!

Word order

Remember that there are three types of word order in German (see page 152). Think carefully about which one to use for each sentence of your translation. Two key rules are:

1 Verb second

Even if there is a time or place expression at the beginning of the sentence, or even an entire subordinate clause, the **verb** always comes second:

I eat vegetables now and again. *Ab und zu* ***esse*** *ich Gemüse.*

In the sentence above, the subject and **verb** have swapped round because the time expression has come first in the sentence.

When my father cooks, we eat vegetables. *Wenn mein Vater kocht,* ***essen*** *wir Gemüse.*

Here, a whole subordinate clause is the first 'idea' of the sentence but the main verb (*essen*) still comes second, after the subordinate clause. Remember to use the 'verb-comma-verb' pattern in this kind of construction.

2 Time – Manner – Place

- Always check that you have included the elements of a sentence in the correct order: 'I eat with my family at home in the evenings'.

Time — Manner

Ich esse abends mit meiner Familie zu Hause.

Place

- Remember to send the verb to the end of the clause after a subordinating conjunction such as *weil*. You must always add a comma before *weil* to indicate the start of the subordinate clause:

We eat meat at the weekend because my sister cooks.	*Am Wochenende essen wir Fleisch,* ***weil*** *meine Schwester* ***kocht****.*

Translation skills

- Be careful with words that can be missed out in English but must be included in German, and vice versa. These can often be learned as set phrases:

We have a dog called Max.	*Wir haben einen Hund,* ***der*** *Max heißt.*
I go **to** school.	*Ich gehe* ***in die*** *Schule.*
On Mondays I have German.	***Montags*** *habe ich Deutsch.*
I would like to be **a teacher**.	*Ich möchte* ***Lehrer/Lehrerin*** *werden.*

- Avoid translating word for word when you translate into German. The present and imperfect tenses are expressed in several ways in English, but just one form is used in German:

  Present: I go / am going to the cinema. → *Ich gehe ins Kino.*

  H Imperfect: I went / was going / used to go to the cinema. → *Ich ging ins Kino.*

  Notice that there are no words for 'am', 'was' or 'used to' in the German translations.

- If you don't know how to say something in German, don't worry too much! Try to think of a synonym (a similar word), or another way to say it using vocabulary that you do know.
- There's a lot to think about when translating into German, but don't panic! Work carefully through each sentence and check your spelling, word order and endings thoroughly to be sure that you have written correct German.

Avoid using translation software. Although online dictionaries can be helpful for translating individual words, there is no guarantee that any online service will provide you with a correct answer in any context.

Notes

Notes